OUTSTANDING BOOKS FOR CHILDREN AND YOUNG PEOPLE

The LA Guide to Carnegie/Greenaway Winners 1937–1997

Keith Barker

LIBRARY ASSOCIATION PUBLISHING
LONDON

© Keith Barker 1998

Published by
Library Association Publishing
7 Ridgmount Street
London WC1E 7AE

Library Association Publishing is wholly owned by The Library Association.

First published 1998

British Library Cataloguing in Publication Data
A catalogue record for this book is available from the British Library.

ISBN 1-85604-287-1

Cover illustration from *Gorilla* © 1983 Anthony Browne.
Reproduced by permission of the publisher, Walker Books Ltd, London.

Typeset from author's disk in 10/13pt Century Schoolbook by Library Association Publishing.
Printed and made in Great Britain by Bookcraft (Bath) Ltd, Midsomer Norton, Somerset.

Contents

List of plates

(Between pages 80 and 81.)

Illustration (p.28) from *Each peach pear plum* by Janet and Allan Ahlberg (Viking, 1978). Copyright © Janet and Allan Ahlberg, 1978.

Illustration from *Gorilla* © 1983 by Anthony Browne.
Reproduced by permission of the publisher, Walker Books Ltd, London.

The baby who wouldn't go to bed, by Helen Cooper. Illustration © Helen Cooper. By arrangement with Transworld Publishers Ltd.

Way home, by Libby Hathorn and Gregory Rogers. Published in Great Britain in 1994 by Andersen Press Ltd, London. First published in 1994 as a Mark Macleod book by Random House Australia.

DEDICATION

To the 1994 selection panel, that 'clutch of strong-minded ladies' who kept me in check, and to Steve because he's special.

Foreword

Encouraging the nation to read and instilling the reading habit in young people is central to the National Year of Reading and a key part of the Government's literacy strategy. I can think of no more appropriate publication to issue at the beginning of the Year of Reading than a celebration of 60 years of some of the best writing for children and young people. The guide should prove invaluable to librarians, teachers and parents. It should help them to introduce to young people the kind of books that will make them lifetime readers. It is an excellent route map through a wondrous and powerful world of literary invention and imagination.

The Rt Hon. David Blunkett MP
Secretary of State for Education and Employment

Introduction

The Library Association's two awards for children's books, the Carnegie Medal and the Kate Greenaway Medal, are important for a number of reasons. They help to provide a microcosm of children's literature mainly in the United Kingdom over the last half of the twentieth century. They help to identify trends of the various eras, from the now mainly forgotten writers of the early period, through to the dominance of a particular publishing house, to developments in the printing of illustrated material, and to the gritty realism of recent winners of the Carnegie Medal. Along the way they pinpoint books of excellence many of which are still available, in order to provide a basis for selection for anyone attempting to produce a collection of worth to young people.

The Carnegie Medal was the first of the two awards to be introduced and it was indeed the first ever British children's book award. Its original concept was that it would be awarded to the best children's book published during the year by a British author and its original intention was to raise standards in a field where the quality of the books in the Victorian and Edwardian periods had declined considerably. The editor of *Library Association record* in announcing the Award hoped that 'librarians and the public feel that they may buy a book that has received the Medal in the certainty that it is in good English, has appropriate imagination, humour and atmosphere, and that it is properly produced from a physical point of view'. This latter aspect was an important element of the Award in a way that is taken for granted by modern selectors as can be seen from this citation of an early winner: 'The format of *The radium woman* is satisfactory. The print is clear, the margins wide and the binding serviceable'. One of the architects of the Award, W.C. Berwick Sayers, set out the criteria for selection. He said the winner should be 'a book for a child somewhere between the ages of nine and twelve, but need not be absolutely within these age limits'. As far as literary quality was concerned 'it should be in the best English; its story should follow the line of the possible, if not the probable; its characters should be alive, its situations credible, and its tone in keeping with the generally accepted standards of good behaviour and right thinking'.

The method by which the early winners were selected was to poll a number of library authorities asking for their votes which were then collated. This was quickly followed (as was the substitution of 'an outstanding book' for 'best book') by an arrangement whereby the winner was selected by a small committee. However, none of the members of that committee were working in the growing area of children's librarianship and the Association of Children's Librarians, the forerunner of the Youth Libraries Group, felt most strongly that children's librarians should be represented on the selection panel. It was to be a number of years before this happened and a number of decades before the selection panel consisted solely of children's librarians. More formal written criteria were introduced which have not changed much in principle over the years. It was felt that 'every member of the committee should be prepared to read all the recommended books on the final list' which at the time consisted of about six books. Considering that current members of the selection committtee have to read and comment on an average of a hundred books on the initial list, it can be seen that the level of commitment expected of committee members has changed quite considerably.

There was also much criticism by children's librarians of the lack of publicity the Award generated. In 1944 Eileen Colwell, the first children's librarian on the selection committee, complained that 'surely if the Award is worth anything, if it is to be a fitting memorial to the benefactor whose name it bears, it should arouse widespread public interest. It needs to be written and talked about, advertised in all libraries and bookshops and awarded with some ceremony'. This appeared to fall on deaf ears for the Award continued to be quietly announced in *Library Association record*, presented to the recipient in The Library Association Council and then forgotten. Not even the announcement of a further medal for children's book illustration, the Kate Greenaway Medal, generated a significant amount of interest.

There had been talk sometime of creating another medal for illustration (indeed the editor of *Junior bookshelf* had suggested one to be named after George Cruikshank) when the Carnegie Medal was introduced. In fact it was another Victorian artist who gave her name to the new medal, founded with little enthusiasm by The Library Association which was still not putting a great deal of effort into promoting either award. However, the twenty first anniversary of the awarding of the Carnegie in 1957 did provoke some interest with a gala lunch (to which the Royal family was invited but declined to attend) and the publication of the first edition of *Chosen for children*, compiled by Marcus Crouch but not to bear his name until the third edition. The two medals held sway as the only British children's book awards until the introduction of the *Guardian* Award a decade later.

One aspect of this period was the dominance of a single publishing house, Oxford University Press, which consistently over this time featured strongly in both awards. The publishing house had provided writers of a high standard and had encouraged developments in the production of illustrated books so it was not surprising that they should reap the rewards. The fact that many members of the selection panel had been on it for some time would also suggest a consistency in the types of book chosen; it was also inevitable that their choices would not all find universal favour. Nevertheless, no other publishing house has dominated the Medals to the same extent since, although in recent years some, such as Walker Books, have achieved a continuous series of winners with a particular type of book, while at least one editor, Jane Nissen at Hamish Hamilton, saw her authors win the Carnegie Medal four years running.

The inevitable backlash came because events were changing, both in the world of children's books and in children's librarianship. Controversy surrounded the Carnegie Medal awards and, to a far lesser extent, the Kate Greenaway awards). Children's books were beginning to reflect the world of their readers in a much more realistic manner, while children's librarians were beginning to seek out previously neglected audiences for the books on their shelves. There was bound to be a feeling that what had gone before was tired and fustian, despite the fact that in their day some of those books had often been regarded as breaking new ground and even in some cases revolutionary. A lively correspondence, which burst into print in the *Times literary supplement*, opened the debate to a wider audience and some changes were introduced: the selection panel, through the use of Youth Libraries Group members, began to reflect the feelings of more children's librarians, while the terms of reference for a writer hoping to win the Medal more than once were clarified, though in the event this has really only taken place infrequently and in the 1980s and 1990s.

By the mid-1970s the selection process had established a pattern still much still in operation. The selection committee consists of librarians who are involved with the Youth Libraries Group. They meet several times, initially to draw up a shortlist of titles from a long list of around a hundred, nominated by members of the Library Association. The shortlisted books are then re-read and the committee reconvenes for a final selection meeting. This is an important aspect of the Award. The

Carnegie and Kate Greenaway Medals are the only British children's book awards selected solely by professionals, most of whom will be working daily with children. This is an element often noted by the winners who appreciate its importance. The fact that the selectors are librarians and that the two medals pioneered British children's book awards is something of which the library profession should be justly proud.

However, criticism could justifiably be made of the lack of publicity that the Awards generate. Eileen Colwell clearly felt it as her comments already quoted show. In 1991 this matter was improved by the first sponsorship of the Medals by Peters Library Service, the children's book suppliers, who continued to sponsor the Awards for the next seven years. Despite the initial concerns of some librarians, this development did not 'cheapen' the Awards but instead helped to raise their profile as, for the first time, it was possible to hire a publicist able to achieve a good deal of press and media coverage. This was accompanied by the introduction of the shadowing process whereby children could set up their own selection process and vote on the shortlist, promoting interest in the difference between selections made by adults and children. Often these have been remarkably similar, helping in some way to dispel the belief that Carnegie winners are the 'great unread', as they were once described.

Looking back over the half-century of the Awards, is it possible to say there is a typical Carnegie or Kate Greenaway Medal winner? The answer is probably 'no' although both awards have their distinctive characteristics. The Carnegie is more likely to go to a novel written for an older audience. Attempts have been made to alleviate this by introducing a second award solely for teenage literature but it is usually regarded as inevitable that an adult selection panel will choose a book with more sophisticated intentions, almost always a novel. Non-fiction has featured very little in the Award and has dated much more quickly than fiction. Poetry rarely appears. The Kate Greenaway Medal by contrast will almost certainly go to a picture book. Books with line drawings have sometimes appeared in the final list but their number has decreased over the years. The danger with this award is that the consideration that a book works well with children could outweigh other considerations and selection committees have to avoid this as strenuously as possible.

This does not answer the question 'What makes a good children's book?' Many critics have dedicated considerable amounts of space to attempting to answer this question so any effort to answer in a short space such as this is bound to be limited. However, the books in this category, diverse though they are, share a number of characteristics. Firstly, they are created by those who have a need to communicate with children. They have not been produced to fit into a strait-jacketed format with a requisite number of words or pages. Often they have been produced with the guidance of a caring and committed editor and production team who care about the quality of the work and how it should be presented. These books have been created by a writer or illustrator who cares deeply about his or her audience, but who wishes to present the story in a way which will not underestimate the intelligence of the child reader, and which will not be designed to appeal only to its lowest common denominator. These books are not written merely to please but to produce a variety of reactions from their readers, who may have been totally unaware that they were capable of responding to books in this way. Many will have been written to help children understand the world which surrounds them and to guide them through to their lives as potential adults. But, above all, they have been created to give pleasure, to produce laughter and tears and to provide a satisfying and rounded whole in a way that is still the hallmark of good children's books.

This book has been written for a number of reasons. The first is that both Awards are of considerable historical interest. Some of the early winners and commended books are still in print but many have disappeared and it is important to consider why they may have been regarded as having merit in their time. (Of course, there is always the problem of the publication date of the winner. Historically, the Awards are announced and presented in the middle of the year after the year in which the books are published. This is why the title of this book explains that Awards made in the years 1937–1997 are listed. However, the books were actually published in the previous year in each case, hence the list of winners is arranged to start at 1936 and end in 1996.)

The other important reason for publishing this book is that it brings together titles of excellence and may therefore act as an ideal selection tool for those hoping to provide for children the best of (mainly) British publishing. Entries have therefore been headed with as much bibliographical information as possible. A typical heading would be:

Gregory Rogers. *Way home* **[text by Libby Hathorn] (Andersen) Andersen 0 86264 541 7; Red Fox 0 09 948681 4**

or:

Author. Title [the writer of the text if different from the main author] (the original publisher) British editions in print at April 1998, with ISBNs.

Note that some editions such as big books, miniatures and some educational editions have not been included. Full details are not always available.

It is surprising that so many of the books on the list, even recent ones, are no longer in print. Another feature of this book is that publishers could use it to trawl their backlists for books which should be reprinted or published in new editions.

It is hoped, then, that you will be able to see the progress of both awards, celebrate those books which still speak to many children, disagree with some of the choices, although doubtless realizing why they were chosen at the time, and promote and find enormous pleasure in these longest-standing and still greatly respected British children's book awards.

The Carnegie Medal

Winners and commended titles

CARNEGIE MEDAL WINNER 1936

Arthur Ransome. *Pigeon post* (Cape) Cape 0 224 02124 9; Red Fox
0 09 996340 X

It is hardly surprising that Arthur Ransome was the first winner of the
Carnegie Medal. He is one of the few oustanding writers of the 1930s and
has now achieved the status of a classic writer although his popularity
with contemporary children is probably not enormous. Ransome revolu-
tionized the adventure story for children with his series of books set around
the Lake District and involving the different gangs of the Swallows,
Amazons and the Ds. They all appear again in *Pigeon post*, written six
years after *Swallows and Amazons*. The story involves the children's newly
found skills of mining for gold which leads them to outwit a competitor as
well as ending the book by helping to fight a forest fire. As in his other
books, Ransome's skill in characterization is evident: these are real children who have all absorbing enthusiasm for such things as mining and also
in this book, pigeon flying. After the mealy-mouthed collection of children
who inhabited children's books at the turn of the century, these must have
seemed a refreshing change. Perhaps a modern children's writer would not
call a main female character Titty but the feelings and highly individually
sketched characteristics of each of the children make the books in the
series still highly accessible to modern children. The books also give a huge
amount of practical information about surviving in the countryside in a
non-didactic way. It was most important that the first Medal should go to
a writer like Arthur Ransome and for the next decade or so the Medal often
went to a book not necessarily for its quality but more for the writer's contribution to the world of children's books in previous years. Ransome, inci-
dentally, was less than impressed by the ceremony at which he received his
Medal: he said it would have been better 'to send the blessed thing by post'.

SECOND PLACE

Howard Spring. *Sampson's circus* (Faber)

This was the only year that a first, second and third choice were
announced. The selection was very much gender orientated with the winner likely to win appreciation from both sexes whereas *Sampson's circus* is
very much a book for boys and the third choice more for girls. It is set in
the circus with most of the main characters being adults. The most appealing is Charlie Chaffinch, a man-of-all-work to Sampson, and who hopes to

become a prize fighter. The two eleven year old boys around whom the story is written become involved in a mystery but the book is also told with a good deal of humour.

THIRD PLACE

Noel Streatfeild. *Ballet shoes* **(Dent) Dent 0 460 06821 0; Puffin 0 14 030041 4, 0 14 036459 5**

This was the first children's book by this prolific author and was an adaptation of a book she wrote for adults. It is still very popular and, although firmly set in its period, has lost none of its charm and good humour. Pauline, Petrova and Posy Fossil, all wards of Matthew Brown, are stagestruck and become involved with a ballet school run by Madame, one of many sharply characterized portraits. The children are not mere ciphers, however: each has her own individual personality. *Ballet shoes* remains one of Streatfeild's most popular books and indeed is still in print, unlike her Medal-winning book, *The circus is coming.*

CARNEGIE MEDAL WINNER 1937

Eve Garnett. *The family from One End Street* **(Muller) Heinemann Educational 0 435 12004 2; Puffin 0 14 036775 6**

If it was not surprising that the first Medal went to a highly respected and established writer like Arthur Ransome, it was probably more of a surprise that the second Medal should go to a new writer and to a book that in its day was almost revolutionary. *The family from One End Street*, which looks at the lives of the children of a dustman and a washerwoman, was the precursor of the realistic novels of the 1960s and 1970s which attempted to show children's lives as they were really lived, rather than an idealized version of a middle class existence. However, Eve Garnett performs her task with a great deal more charm than many of her successors, which may explain why the book has remained extremely popular. The writer trained as an artist and her pencil sketches decorate the pages of the novel. She did some drawings of children in London's East End and decided to write a story about some of the children she was drawing. The Ruggles have a large family and in each chapter one of the children has an escapade. These are not huge, world shattering events but the cosy, everyday happenings of a very ordinary family. That is their appeal. Perhaps from today's viewpoint the book shares an unconsciously patronizing view of the working classes with the films and plays of that period. However, the skill and charm of the stories, coupled with the drawings by the author, help to keep the family alive. Strangely, despite the popularity of the family story as a genre, few have been Medal winners. *The family from One End Street* was published in the same year as another modern classic, Tolkein's *The hobbit*. Which was the more worthy of being a Medal winner?

CARNEGIE MEDAL WINNER 1938

Noel Streatfeild. *The circus is coming* (Dent)

Noel Streatfeild was in contention for the first Medal so it is hardly surprising that she should soon appear as a Medal winner. Like Eve Garnett's, her stories are always deeply rooted in realism and none more so than in this book where, despite its glamorous subject matter, there is a strong feeling of pragmatism in the author's descriptions of the hard work each day undertaken by the performers, which must partly be due to the author's research before she wrote the book. Two very spoilt and snobbish children, Peter and Santa, become orphans on their aunt's death and run away to find their uncle in a circus, rather than face life in an orphanage. Here, they learn the value of hard work and humility. Along the way, we meet a fascinating collection of characters, the residents of Cob's Circus. Noel Streatfeild's books are still read by children, although it is more likely to be those connected with ballet. This, and the fact that circuses, particularly those which involve performing animals, as Cob's is, are frowned on, probably means that this book will be read only by a minority of children. However, the sheer sweep of the story and the liveliness of its characters would be attractive to those prepared to make the attempt. The choice of *The circus is coming* was controversial at the time, particularly when children's librarians discovered that only two members of the selection committee attended the meeting when it was chosen.

CARNEGIE MEDAL WINNER 1939

Eleanor Doorly. *The radium woman* (Heinemann)

As will be seen, non-fiction does not figure largely among the winners of the Medal and indeed not much within the commended categories. There are valid reasons for this. Knowledge changes dramatically in even a short space of time so if a book is to be a likely contender for the Medal, its subject matter has to be likely to remain static for some time. Again, methods of presenting information also change significantly, far more so than the presentation of fiction which remains relatively timeless. Those non-fiction titles that have won the Award are extremely unlikely to be read by even a few children today, to an even greater extent than books by, for example, Eve Garnett or Noel Streatfeild. Where non-fiction probably has a stronger chance of survival is in the field of biography: indeed it was a biography of Marie Curie that has the distinction of being the first non-fiction Medal winner. Based on the scientist's own autobiography, *The radium woman* tells of Manya Sklodovska's upbringing in Poland, her escape to Paris to work and her marriage to Pierre Curie. The discovery of radium is told in an enthralling way and the book ends with the deaths of the two scientists, Marie's through the very radium she has discovered. Much of this is told in an absorbing way, restrained but imaginative. This year also denoted a significant step in the history of the Medal itself for it was the first time Eileen Colwell sat on the selection committee, the first children's librarian to do so. She was to remain on the committee for over twenty years.

CARNEGIE MEDAL WINNER 1940

Kitty Barne. *Visitors from London* (Dent)

Some Medal winners are timeless and some belong very much to their period. The first Medal winner of the war years is in the latter category and indeed was the first Carnegie Medal winner to go out of print, so topical was its subject matter. *Visitors from London* looks at the effect a group of evacuees has on a village, a topic which was popular again some decades after the end of the war. What distinguishes those later books from Kitty Barne's work is that the later novels looked at the viewpoint of the evacuees themselves whereas Barne takes an outsider's look at the working class families who invaded the leafy middle class suburbs. The children of the London slums who accept the ways of the countryside are regarded with approval whereas those who yearn for the urban lifestyle are treated with derision and contempt. This was no doubt the feeling of many at the time (as can be seen from the films of the period) but it really makes *Visitors from London* a piece for historical interest only and a warning to future selectors to look for something other than topicality when awarding prizes.

CARNEGIE MEDAL WINNER 1941

Mary Treadgold. *We couldn't leave Dinah* **(Cape)**

There could hardly be a greater contrast between this book and the previous year's winner, *Visitors from London*. Although *We couldn't leave Dinah* is very much of its own period, having as its main theme the invasion of the Channel Islands by the Germans, its sweep and drive carry it along, dispelling any infelicities similar to those which disturb a reading of Kitty Barne's book. Caroline and Mick Templeton are on holiday on the island of Clerinel when news comes of the invasion. As for many children, this occurrence at first seems too remote to be important and its main effect is that it distracts Caroline from her activities in the pony club. Accidentally left behind on the island, they are forced to hide in a cave until, after a number of adventures, the island's resistance movement manages to get them on a destroyer and to safety. *We couldn't leave Dinah* combines two popular genres: the adventure story and the pony story. Episodes such as the children's flight to the port, only to be left on the quay, and Caroline's love and devotion for Dinah, her pony, are thrillingly described. Neither does the author provide any easy solutions in the plotting of the adventure aspect. The children manage to achieve through their own quick wit and courage. Mary Treadgold herself seemed surprised at winning the Medal and said she wondered 'what quiet book, what book with a less obviously popular appeal was overlooked that year'.

CARNEGIE MEDAL WINNER 1942

'BB' (Denys Watkins-Pitchford). *The little grey men* **(Eyre & Spottiswoode)**

This story of the last gnomes of England is the first fantasy title to appear as a Medal winner and it was still popular until recent times. Three gnomes, Sneezewort, Baldmoney and Dodder, sail upstream in search of Cloudberry, their missing brother. Along the way they encounter adventures with the wildlife which lives along the stream, and tackle the gamekeeper. They achieve all that they do through ingenuity and their knowledge of the countryside, not by any magical means. Like a later winner, Mary Norton's *The borrowers*, this is the human world scaled down and is imbued with the author's deep and evident love for the countryside. The gnomes each have their own personality, as do the various animals and birds which inhabit the woods the gnomes travel through. The book is also enhanced by the author's own scraperboard illustrations which help to preserve the charm and quirkiness of the text. 'BB' went on to write a succession of novels set within this world but *The little grey men* was probably the best of them.

1943: No award was made in this year

Carnegie Medal winner 1944

Eric Linklater. *The wind on the moon* (Macmillan)

Poet and novelist Linklater's novel is a piece of whimsy typical of a style extremely popular in the middle of the twentieth century. It has serious undertones but they are portrayed in such a cloud of froth that they do not threaten to overtake the story. It concerns two naughty sisters, Dinah and Dorinda, whose father has been taken to a dictator's castle in middle Europe. A wind blew on the moon the night he disappears, which helps to explain their naughtiness. However, they have reformed sufficiently towards the end of the book to set off in search of him, accompanied by a variety of zany characters. There is a touch of Thurber or Osbert Lancaster in the writing. Despite his renown as a writer of adult books, Linklater does not write down to children. Although the setting is timeless, there are echoes of what was happening in the world at the time the book was written. It is not a particularly dated book, despite having a governess as a key character, but its own particular whimsy may work against it in the eyes of modern children.

1945: No award was made in this year

Carnegie Medal winner 1946

Elizabeth Goudge. *The little white horse* (University of London Press) Lion 0 7459 1458 6

The little white horse is also a fantasy but here the emphasis is on charm and goodness but with little sentimentality. The story is an allegory but the vividness of the characterization and the excitement of its telling help to sugar the pill. The heroine, Maria, is particularly strongly drawn as she attempts to bring harmony to the disparate characters who inhabit the village of Silverydew. Many of them are depicted as eccentrics and outside the norm, a trait which always appeals to the tastes of child readers. Elizabeth Goudge was also a successful writer for adults and one of the hallmarks of her writing is her belief in the essential goodness of people. *The little white horse* is a most charming and delightful example of an unmawkish way of showing this goodness.

CARNEGIE MEDAL WINNER 1947

Walter de la Mare. *Collected stories for children* (Faber)

This was the first of a number of awards made in the next decade when the selection panel recognized writers as much for their past achievements as for the particular book which received the Medal. Similar awards went in later years to Eleanor Farjeon and C. S. Lewis although only one of the stories in de la Mare's book was new. This prompted *Junior bookshelf* to question whether, if A. A. Milne's *When we were very young* were reprinted, it also might be a Medal winner. Walter de la Mare was a great stylist, hugely admired in his day both for his poetry and his prose writing; some of his work is still admired and may be due for reassessment. All the stories in this collection are polished and accomplished and, with a skilled reader, would without doubt capture the attention of many children. But an adult mediator is definitely needed. Very few modern children would automatically pick this book up for themselves. Nevertheless there is great variety in the stories, whether they are chilling examples like *The riddle* or retellings of traditional motifs like *Dick and the beanstalk*. And behind them all is de la Mare's clear sighted conception of what childhood entails.

CARNEGIE MEDAL WINNER 1948

Richard Armstrong. *Sea change* (Dent)

This is a book intentionally written for boys in order to acquaint them with the gruelling but often exciting life in the merchant navy. Its two main protagonists, Cam and Rusty, are apprentices with very different characters. Rusty is methodical whereas Cam is impatient and does not see the point of everyday routine on board ship. However, a series of events helps to teach him the value of routine as an essential part of work at sea and that slapdash and impatient work can cause accidents. All this is told in a style direct and without frills. The writer describes a number of exciting events such as a fire at sea but his main concern is with his downbeat and (for the time) graphic descriptions of life on board ship. Admittedly *Sea change* is in an old fashioned tradition: a boys' adventure story in the style of Rider Haggard, although without Edwardian imperialist trappings, but it still provides a good deal of excitement.

CARNEGIE MEDAL WINNER 1949

Agnes Allen. *The story of your home* **(Faber)**

The best non-fiction books are those which stand out from the norm, sometimes despite the best intentions of publishers. There is a limited number of non-fiction titles where the author has tried to do something different and *The story of your home* is early example of one such. Agnes Allen attempts to tell the history of houses through narrative, concentrating on those who have lived in them, what they wore and how they lived, rather than looking at them as architecture. This makes it far more interesting for young readers than if it were a dry account of historical fact. The author has obviously researched her subject well but takes care not to overwhelm the reader with too much detail and is selective in what she presents. As with the other non-fiction titles in the Carnegie list, it is unlikely that modern children, used as they are to the ubiquitous full colour double page spread, will find the book immediately appealing but it still has merit: a selective mediator may find it an ideal introduction to the subject.

CARNEGIE MEDAL WINNER 1950

Elfrida Vipont. *The lark on the wing* **(Oxford University Press)**

The sequel to *The lark in the morn* is an example of a genre that was to eventually take over the Carnegie Medal: that of the teenage novel. However, as this type of book is almost inevitably rooted in its time, the book is very much a period piece and it is unlikely that many present-day teenagers will be able to empathize with the characters or setting or with the book's two themes of singing and Quakerism. This is a pity because the book does have a great deal to offer apart from a feeling of nostalgia for a period which seems to be much gentler than the present. It tells of Kit Haverard and her attempt to make a career out of her singing. By the end of the book she has grown, both as a person and as a singer and the reader is swept along with all the turmoils she encounters. All this is told in an absorbing way which many would find attractive if they were prepared to overlook the story's period trappings. The year 1950 was also the year of the publication of C. S Lewis's *The lion, the witch and the wardrobe*, a book still widely read today but the selection committee waited until the end of the Narnia saga and the author's much inferior *The last battle* before honouring him.

CARNEGIE MEDAL WINNER 1951

Cynthia Harnett. *The wool-pack* (Methuen) Puffin 0 14 030153 4

Historical novels began to feature prominently among the Medal winners and commended books in the 1950s and 1960s until they began to lose popularity in later decades. Cynthia Harnett was one of the early and most successful exponents of the genre with her richly detailed, but still hugely enjoyable, novels of which *The wool-pack* is one of the best. Set in the Cotswolds in Renaissance England, it follows the life of young Nicholas Fetterlock, the son of a wool merchant. The feeling of place is very strong as the hero attempts to free his father's business from the grips of the Lombard money lenders. Nicholas becomes betrothed to Cecily and the story reveals his growing love for her. With lots of exciting events, it is still essentially a domestic story. The writer's mastery of her research is exemplary for it is not overdrawn on to the main events, thus the child reader will still gain much insight into what life was like at the time.

CARNEGIE MEDAL WINNER 1952

Mary Norton. *The borrowers* (Dent) Heinemann Educational
0 435 12277 0; Puffin 0 14 030110 0, 0 14 036451 X

There is no doubt that the 1952 winner has become a classic and the selection committee is to be congratulated for recognizing its potential early. The premise of the book, that there exists an alternative world of little people in parallel with the everyday world and who live on the borrowings of their larger counterparts, is so simple and so intriguing that it is not surprising that it has engaged the minds and emotions of its readers since, and that it has been televised and filmed to great acclaim. The Borrower family: Pod, Homily and their daughter Arrietty, live behind the clock in a large country house. They are the last remnants of a dying breed though this aspect of the tale, which could have caused it to veer into tragedy, is only lightly touched on. Arrietty feels frustrated that their existence has to be so covert and takes more risks than she should in venturing into the outside world. She does, however, make friends with a little boy in the house who brings them luxurious furniture from a dolls' house until their secret is inevitably discovered and the Borrowers' home destroyed. There are sequels, one of which appears as a commended book in subsequent years of the Medal's history, but it is this first book that captures the feelings of this small but recognizable family with its fascinating and imaginative glimpse into a scaled-down version of our own world.

CARNEGIE MEDAL WINNER 1953

Edward Osmond. *A valley grows up* **(Oxford University Press)**

The author of this depiction of the imaginary town of Dungate through seventy centuries is also the illustrator: the book began life as a sequence of oil paintings to which he added a text. This is a history lesson, told in a palatable manner, which uses the development of the town and its surrounding countryside as a lesson in landscape change and social history. All this is depicted in a leisurely and unaffected manner which grabs the reader's attention effortlessly. It is difficult in some ways to separate the text from the illustrations and indeed if it were published today, it would more likely be a contender for the Emil Award designed to mark those books where text and illustration blend seamlessly together. It should be remembered that this was the period when members of the selection committee were beginning to pressurize The Library Association into establishing a separate award for illustrated books; without wishing to denigrate Edward Osmond's text too much, it could be suggested that this book may have been more of a political than an aesthetic winner.

CARNEGIE MEDAL WINNER 1954

Ronald Welch. *Knight crusader* **(Oxford University Press)**

This is an adventure story set in times of the Crusades; although much of it is rooted in realism, and the author does not shirk from describing the real horrors of fighting and the difference in manners between the sophisticated Eastern knights and the brutish Europeans, it carries with it all the trappings of the historical adventure yarn. Philip is of Norman lineage and gets involved in the march on Damascus which was the beginning of the Third Crusade. Along the way he meets King Richard, whose character the author successfully brings to life. The climax of the story finds Philip in his home town in Wales, returning to claim his inheritance. There is enough action here to satisfy those readers who thrill to the stories of Robin Hood and Ivanhoe but also enough skill in the writing to attract those more thoughtful readers who demand more subtlety from their reading matter.

SPECIAL COMMENDATION

Kathleen Lines. *Lavender's blue* (Oxford University Press) Oxford University Press 0 19 279537 6, 0 19 272208 5

This was the first year that commendations were introduced, a method whereby the merits of those titles not quite of Medal-winning quality could be recognized. The names of future Medal winners frequently appeared in these lists, often in an apprentice-like manner, before their work received the ultimate accolade. *Lavender's blue* is an unusual choice for a special commendation as it is not original work but a sequence of nursery rhymes edited by Katheen Lines. It is more likely that the selection committee wished to honour the artwork of Harold Jones but was unable to find an alternative way of doing so as The Library Association was still dragging its heels over the introduction of an award for illustration. Harold Jones is one of the most neglected of children's book illustrators of the time. His work combines both a simplicity and a sophistication which makes his work stand above that of his contemporaries, as is highly evident in this book. The following year the Kate Greenaway Medal was introduced: it is interesting to speculate that, had it been awarded in this year, Harold Jones would probably have been its first recipient.

COMMENDED

L. M. Boston. *The children of Green Knowe* (Faber) Puffin 0 14 030789 3, 0 14 036461 7

The house of Green Knowe had a considerable influence on children's literature over the next decade as Lucy Boston continued to tell stories based around the house where she lived. This particular book is a sequence of magical stories where the little boy, Toby, manages to communicate with his ancestors and, along with his horse Feste, is transported into different times. The writing is quietly persuasive and fragile and is more for the thoughtful and sophisticated reader.

Nicholas Stuart Gray. *Over the hills to Fabylon* **(Oxford University Press)**

A comic fairy tale by a writer better known for his children's plays. Related in 15 progressive episodes, it tells of King Francis of Fabylon and his troublesome family. Suitable mainly for child readers who appreciate parody, it is likely to have a limited appeal.

C. S. Lewis. *The horse and his boy* **(Bodley Head) Armada 0 00 671666 0; Collins 0 00 183182 8, 0 00 674035 9**

This is one of the sequence of books set around the mythical land of Narnia, a sequence which begins with *The lion, the witch and the wardrobe*. Shasta discovers that Arsheesh the fisherman is not his real father and Bree, the talking horse, persuades him to run away across the great desert to the safe, free land of Narnia, where High King Peter rules. Along the way he has a series of breathtaking adventures. *The horse and his boy* is of the same quality as the others in the Narnia sequence, as two years later the selection panel was to recognize by awarding the Medal to the final book in the series, *The last battle*.

Barbara Leonie Picard. *The lady of the Linden Tree* **(Oxford University Press)**

This is a sequence of 12 stories based in the folklore tradition, full of chivalry and knights and told with charm and style.

James Reeves. *English fables and fairy stories* **(Oxford University Press) Oxford University Press 0 19 274137 3**

A collection of nineteen traditional tales, some well known and others more obscure. They have a distinctive feel, mainly as a result of the author's voice; he does not attempt to hide the violence of many of these traditional stories.

Rosemary Sutcliff. *The eagle of the Ninth* **(Oxford University Press) Puffin 0 14 030890 3, 0 14 036457 9**

Rosemary Sutcliff, one of the greatest twentieth century children's writers, appears many times in the Carnegie lists. *The eagle of the Ninth* is one of her most successful books. Set in one of Sutcliff's most frequently used periods, the Roman invasion, it tells of Marcus Flavius Aquila who sets out to retrieve the lost eagle standard of the Ninth Legion in the unknown territory of Ultima Thule. It is told with Rosemary Sutcliff's special blend of empathy with the chosen period and great storytelling skills.

CARNEGIE MEDAL WINNER 1955

Eleanor Farjeon. *The little bookroom* **(Oxford University Press)**

This was another of those awards made not so much for the quality of the book itself but more for the contribution the writer had made to twentieth century children's literature. Eleanor Farjeon cannot be denied her place as, over the decades, she had helped to improve both the quality of writing for children and the way children should be regarded as equals and not a group to whom it was so easy to talk down. *The little bookroom* is a sequence of 27 stories, written over 30 years. All bear Eleanor Farjeon's characteristic lightness of touch and rely very much on magic and a certain benign outlook on life. The selection committee felt, correctly in retrospect, that it would be the last opportunity it would have 'to recognize appropriately the work of one of the major writers for children of this century'.

COMMENDED

Lancelot Hogben. *Man must measure* **(Rathbone)**

This large-format non-fiction book tells the story of mathematics in an approachable and attractive manner.

Margaret Jowett. *Candidate for fame* **(Oxford University Press)**

A rollicking yarn about theatrical life in the late eighteenth century which includes famous people from that period but whose main story involves Deborah Keate and her progress from a child actress in Yorkshire to one of Drury Lane's stars. The mood is atmospheric, with a great deal of period feel.

Jo Manton. *The story of Albert Schweitzer* **(Methuen)**

The famous missionary was still alive when this biography was produced. It traces with understanding and sympathy a life which in early childhood was shaped and dedicated to the service of humanity. The major part of the book tells of Schweitzer's preparatory life in Europe until his first journey to Africa in 1913.

William Mayne. *A swarm in May* **(Oxford University Press)**
Hodder 0 340 65681 6

William Mayne's name was another which would figure prominently over the years in the commended, and finally the winner's, lists. He is still one of the major figures in children's books and, unlike most other writers of this period, is still producing a significant number of high quality works. *A swarm in May* is one in a sequence of chorister stories. In the cathedral, there is a tradition of beekeeping and singing and of bringing the cathedral bees to be blessed while an introit is sung. The book's hero, John Owen, is not much interested in the singing but he enjoys keeping bees. How this conflict is resolved is told with an assured touch.

Philippa Pearce. *Minnow on the Say* **(Oxford University Press)**
Oxford University Press 0 19 277064 0, 0 19 271615 8; Puffin
0 14 031022 3

This is the first published work of a writer who was to have a lasting effect on children's books in the latter half of the twentieth century. The Minnow is a canoe which David finds on the River Say. It leads him to Adam who lives in an old, neglected house and to a treasure hunt. Already the quality of Philippa Pearce's writing and her skill in characterization, which reached their finest in the book honoured by the selection committee several years later, *Tom's midnight garden*, is evident.

CARNEGIE MEDAL WINNER 1956

C. S. Lewis. *The last battle* **(Bodley Head) Armada 0 00 671669 5;**
Collins 0 00 184441 5, 0 00 674036 7

C. S. Lewis's Narnia series has long been recognized as one of the high points of twentieth century literature and it is not surprising that the

Carnegie selection committee wished to mark Lewis's achievement. In some ways it is unfortunate that it was not recognized earlier, for *The last battle*, the final book in the saga, is the one generally regarded as the weakest in the series. The whole ethos of the books is the struggle between good, shown most distinctly through the figure of Aslan, the Christ-like lion, and evil, depicted in each of the books through a number of characters. Some have baulked at Lewis's Christian allegory and his didactic writing but children are often persuaded by the attractive characterization and the theme of much fantasy, the conflicts in many humans between what they know to be good and what they are attracted to as evil. In the final book of the saga, evil does appear to be triumphant but Lewis provides an epilogue in which he points to the mysticism of the land of Narnia itself. Those who have read the rest of the series will of course wish to finish it with this book but may be disappointed that it does not have the deft skill of many of the others.

COMMENDED

Rumer Godden. *The fairy doll* (Macmillan)

This is one of Rumer Godden's stories for younger children. A Christmas tale, it describes how clumsy, naughty and not very clever Elizabeth is convinced that the fairy on top of the Christmas tree has stitching on her shoes which is carried out by fairy mice. Elizabeth is an interesting creation, the youngest child who is very different from her siblings, and her story is most convincingly told by this highly regarded writer.

William Mayne. *Chorister's cake* (Oxford University Press) Jade 0 903461 41 2

William Mayne. *The member for the Marsh* (Oxford University Press)

The first book is the sequel to *A swarm in May* and is another cathedral story. The central character, Sandwell, fights a solitary war against school tradition and discipline. There is also the background theme of rivalry between the two halves of the choir which culminates on Guy Fawkes Night. *The member for the Marsh* tells of four individual boys, the Harmonious Mud Stickers, and is set in Somerset. The four carry out a number of schoolboy pranks and accept a shy new recruit. Both books are intelligently written with skill and ingenuity.

Barbara Leonie Picard. *Ransom for a knight* **(Oxford University Press)**

Barbara Leonie Picard was one of a significant group of writers of historical novels at this time. Their aim was to make history as realistic as possible so that one can almost smell the trappings of medieval England in this novel. It also contains a plucky heroine, Alys de Renneville, who sets off with a young servant boy, Hugh, to carry across England a ransom intended to free her father and brother from the Scots. Along the way they encounter a variety of sharply drawn characters, most notably the witch Maudlin.

Ian Serraillier. *The silver sword* **(Cape) Heinemann Educational 0 435 12039 5; Puffin 0 14 030146 1, 0 14 036452 8**

This has become such a popular book for use in schools that many children will remember it as a minor classic. Set at the time of the end of the Second World War, it itells of the occupation of Poland where the three Balicki children are attempting to survive without their parents. With the aid of the sharply drawn orphan, Jan, they make their way towards Switzerland to freedom and hopefully a reunion with their mother and father. The silver sword (in reality a paper knife) becomes a talisman for them. Considered by some adults at the time to be too realistic, *The silver sword* is still a powerful testament to the strength and survival of innocent casualties of war.

Rosemary Sutcliff. *The shield ring* **(Oxford University Press) Puffin 0 14 034969 3**

All of this writer's skills in evoking the past are evident in this telling of the story of the shield ring which is the main defence in the last Viking stronghold in the heights of the land we now know as the Lake District of England. This is another of Sutcliff's powerful and highly readable books.

CARNEGIE MEDAL WINNER 1957

William Mayne. *A grass rope* **(Oxford University Press)**

William Mayne's name appeared so frequently in the Medal commendations that it was only a matter of time before he was awarded the Medal itself. Mayne has always been a difficult writer to categorize: to many his work is difficult but to a significant minority it follows in the long tradition of quality British writing for children. He is an uncompromising writer who treats his readers as equals and who is not prepared to sacrifice his own high standards for easy popularity. *A grass rope* is typical of much of his work. Set in Yorkshire where the writer still lives, it tells of how an ordinary farming family becomes involved in the ways of magic. Mary, the owner of the grass rope, still believes in fairies and this belief helps her and Adam Forrest, the grammar school head boy, to solve the mystery of the lost hounds of Thoradale. This is a quiet type of magic but is no less powerfully evoked for that. It is difficult to distinguish this book from the high standard of quality writing that has poured from Mayne's pen over the years. He is indeed still winning prizes as is evidenced by his being given the Emil Award in 1997 for *Lady Muck*.

COMMENDED

Gillian Avery. *The warden's niece* (Collins)

This was Gillian Avery's first novel for children and it is set, as her other books generally are, in her beloved Victorian times. In 1875 Maria, the attractively portrayed heroine, begins a new school. Her ambition is to become a professor but she seems to be thwarted when she is forced to wear a label marked 'slut' for drawing a map of Germany. All this is told in a lively and hugely enjoyable way.

Anne Barrett. *Songbird's grove* (Collins)

A novel which was realistic in its period, this is a story of its period, involving as it does a 'teddy boy' gang. A smiling, enigmatic stone head is found in the rubble of a London garden. Martin who has recently moved to the city would like to restore the head but faces the resistance of the gang in doing so.

Antonia Forest. *Falconer's lure* (Faber)

Antonia Forest wrote a sequence of books involving the Marlow family which was highly regarded at this time and which is still fondly remembered with nostalgia by some. In this particular book some members of the family are involved in falconry, an involvement which also coincides with their move from London to the country.

William Mayne. *The blue boat* **(Oxford University Press)**

Two imaginative brothers on holiday with a strict adult discover a hidden mere and island, where they appear to enter a world of giants and goblins. The explanation is simple: the apparitions are off-duty circus performers.

Katharine Savage. *The story of the Second World War* **(Oxford University Press)**

This is a straightforward account of World War Two. It describes the pattern of events which led to war and the heroism of ordinary men and women as well as the forces in the war. It encompasses descriptions both of battles and of what was going on in the United Kingdom, all in a briskly told narrative.

Rosemary Sutcliff. *The silver branch* **(Oxford University Press)**
Puffin 0 14 031221 8

Described in Rosemary Sutcliff's typically absorbing manner, this is the sequel to *The eagle of the ninth*. Flavius, a descendant of Marcus Flavius Aquila from the previous book, finds the mutilated standard. In the meantime his cousin Justin, a young surgeon in the Roman army, discovers a plot to overthrow the emperor Carausius.

CARNEGIE MEDAL WINNER 1958

Philippa Pearce. *Tom's midnight garden* **(Oxford University Press) Oxford University Press 0 19 271128 8, 0 19 271607 7; Puffin 0 14 030893 8, 0 14 036454 4**

Some Carnegie Medal winners are hotly disputed but there are a few about which there is absolutely no doubt. *Tom's midnight garden* is without doubt one of them. Hailed by critics and readers alike, as recently as 1998 the eminent critic John Rowe Townsend was saying it 'still seems to me to be the outstanding British children's book of the half-century'. Tom is sent to stay with relatives while his brother is recuperating from measles. He is bored by the old house until one night he hears the clock striking 13. He finds he is able to travel back to a time where he meets the lonely orphan girl, Hatty. The final pieces of the jigsaw are completed in the emotionally powered climax where Tom meets other members of the household. This is told with an assured and deft touch which immediately attracts the attention of the reader and then produces a moving denouement which reduces most readers to tears.

COMMENDED

L. M. Boston. *The chimneys of Green Knowe* **(Faber) Puffin 0 14 030840 7**

Another in Lucy Boston's series of stories (see p.13) based around the setting of her Tudor mansion. In this one, Tolly, who has come to stay in the Easter holidays, patches together the lives of the Oldnow family, just as his great-grandmother is mending a patchwork quilt.

Rosemary Sutcliff. *Warrior scarlet* **(Oxford University Press)**

This is set in the Bronze age. Adolescent boys have to carry out the wolf test which involves killing a wolf unaided, entitling them to wear the warrior scarlet, the symbol of manhood. For Drem, who is crippled in one arm, this test holds special terrors.

CARNEGE MEDAL WINNER 1959

Rosemary Sutcliff. *The lantern bearers* **(Oxford University Press) Puffin 0 14 031222 6**

Rosemary Sutcliff was one of those writers whose name had appeared on the commended lists so often that it was hardly surprising that she eventually became a Medal winner. This is always a tricky area because some early novels may show such maturity that they are obvious Medal winners whereas others in retrospect are apprentice works that the author betters in later years. However, in this case the selection committee was wise to wait, for *The lantern bearers* demonstrates Rosemary Sutcliff's skills so quintessentially that it would have been churlish to have denied her the Award. It is again set in Roman Britain. Aquila (a character found in other Sutcliff novels) is defending his part of Britain from Saxon invaders. He is captured and forced into thralldom while his sister is compelled to marry one of the tribe's leaders. Aquila escapes and joins Ambrosius's army, becoming one of the last lantern bearers whose job it is to defend against the forces of might. The past is yet again brought vividly to life by a mature and sophisticated writer whose prose style is as absorbing as her characterization.

COMMENDED

Cynthia Harnett. *The load of unicorn* (Methuen)

Another historical novel, this time centred around the world of Caxton. Its basis is the paper scriveners who made a living by copying books by hand in the fifteenth century and who attempt to conceal a load of paper from Caxton. Bendy, the young hero, tries to protect him. Cynthia Harnett's style may not be as appealing as that of some of her contemporaries but the book is highly enjoyable nevertheless.

Mary Norton. *The borrowers afloat* (Dent) Puffin 0 14 030458 4

The third in the Borrowers series, in this book the tiny family set off for Little Fordham, an area with a model village. They travel down the river, encountering a number of adventures along the way. While not being able to completely reproduce the freshness of the original, the story is still inventive enough and the characters still sufficiently attractive to make this a very amusing and delightful read.

Margery Sharp. *The rescuers* (Collins)

The plot of this book is probably better known in its Walt Disney manifestation. Three mice, the pampered Miss Bianca, the good-hearted kitchen boy Bernard and the sturdy sailor mouse Nils, set out on a rescue mission to save a poor, languishing poet who has been kept in the Black Castle. A delightful and enjoyable romp.

John Verney. *Friday's tunnel* (Collins)

This was the first children's book by the well known adult writer and poet. It concerns two children, Friday and the girl narrator February, who are the children of Augustus Callender, a newspaper correspondent. Their adventure begins with the discovery in the Mediterranean of caprium, a mineral with sinister properties. It is unlikely that modern children would react well to two characters with such arch names but they may get involved in the adventure element of the story.

Andrew Young. *Quiet as moss* **(Hart-Davis)**

This is a collection of 36 poems chosen by Leonard Clark. Andrew Young was a religious poet writing around the middle of the twentieth century and this was the first collection of poetry to appear in the Awards list, apart from the nursery rhyme selection *Lavender's blue*. Poetry is a genre which rarely features in them.

CARNEGIE MEDAL WINNER 1960

I. W. Cornwall. *The making of man* (Phoenix House)

This was the last non-fiction title to win the Award and it is not hard to understand why so few were outright winners, although non-fiction sometimes appears in the commended lists. The presentation of non-fiction is an extremely important element in its success: titles may be refreshed if the illustrations they contain are updated and revised even though the text remains intact. Unfortunately, in the case of *The making of man* the book's presentation makes it seem dated. I. W. Cornwall was a scientist and his lucid text attempts to show young people the progression of humankind from life in caves to modern times. He shows evolution from a Darwinian viewpoint, an aspect vividly amplified in the original illustrations by M. Maitland Howard. The book could be read with pleasure by young people as its central theme is relevant and is explained clearly and lucidly. The *Times educational supplement* Information Book Award, introduced in 1972, now solves the thorny problem about what to do with non-fiction.

COMMENDED

Hester Burton. *The great gale* (Oxford University Press)

Hester Burton was later to make a name for herself as an historical novelist but this book is set in almost contemporary times and is concerned with the floods that affected the Norfolk coast in 1953. Mark and Mary demonstrate their bravery by rescuing others in their rowing boat and taking them to a safe haven, Sir Bartlett Speke's house on top of a hill. A fast-moving adventure story.

Robert Graves. *The penny fiddle* **(Cassell)**

This is a collection of 23 original poems for children by the author *of I Claudius*, beautifully illustrated by Edward Ardizzone.

Frederick Grice. *The bonny pit laddie* **(Oxford University Press)**

A gritty story that tends to be more popular with adults than with young people, this book gained a substantial reputation in the 1960s as a powerful recreation of working-class life at the turn of the century. Dick Ullathorne lives in a mining village near Durham. Sent down the mines at the age of 12 and put in charge of the ponies, a serious accident makes him doubt his future in the pits.

Mary K. Harris *Seraphina* **(Faber)**

This is a coming-of-age story in which the astute Seraphina, a lonely schoolgirl, slowly begins to come to terms with her life and herself. Some pertinent situations which will strike a chord with young adults in particular could well overcome the disadvantage of its period setting.

Ian Serraillier. *The ivory horn* **(Oxford University Press)**

The stories in this book are retold from *The song of Roland*. They tell of the heroes of France who fought the Moslems in Spain under the leadership of Charlemagne. A particularly striking episode tells of the epic battle of the Pass of Roncesvalles. This is a stirring and romantic book, shot through with Serraillier's affinity with the past.

CARNEGIE MEDAL WINNER 1961

L. M. Boston. *A stranger at Green Knowe* **(Faber) Puffin 0 14 030871 7**

Lucy Boston's stories, based around the history of her own home, appeared a number of times in the commended lists of the Award. Told in the writer's distinctive and quietly drawn style, this is the fourth of her books to have Green Knowe as a setting but whereas the others had the past as a vital element, here is a novel set very firmly in the present. The main theme is the relationship between Ping, a Chinese refugee, and

Hanno, an escaped gorilla. This unlikely premise allows the author to draw a series of parallels between the two characters. Ping recognizes why the gorilla should want to escape from a zoo whereas Hanno wishes to look after and protect the displaced Chinese boy. Lucy Boston's account of the ceremony at which she received her Carnegie Medal (which she felt was 'almost exactly like the one I got for swimming the mile when I was eleven') is recounted in her autobiography *Memory in a house* and makes salutary reading.

COMMENDED

Antonia Forest. *Peter's room* (Faber)

This is another story in the books about the Marlows (see p.19), this time set at Christmas, their first at Trennels, their new home. The family acts out an imaginary story based on Emily Brontë's Gondal and Angria sagas. The characters in the story begin to take over, however. Curiously enough the following year's winner, *The twelve and the genii*, has the Brontë sisters' imaginary stories as its central theme.

Rumer Godden. *Miss Happiness and Miss Flower* (Macmillan)

Nona, who has lived in India, is now staying with her cousins. She helps to dispel the strangeness of her new surroundings by building a Japanese house where she creates stories based around her two Japanese dolls. A typically vibrant Rumer Godden story for younger children which uses many of the writer's favourite themes.

James Reeves. *Ragged robin* (Heinemann) Walker 0 7445 1108 9

In far-off times a king falls from grace and sings ragged rhymes to earn his living. Changed into a bird, he continues to sing and the author cleverly provides a rhyme for each letter of the alphabet.

John Verney. *February's road* (Collins)

A sequel to *Friday's tunnel*, a commended title in previous years, the theme of this book is that there is a proposal to build a new trunk road through the Callendar family garden. February is determined to stop the building but this is problematic as the children's father, Augustus, has for a long time been complaining in his newspaper column about the state of the country's road system. Still a topical storyline but modern children may not respond as well to the characterization as previously.

CARNEGIE MEDAL WINNER 1962

Pauline Clarke. *The twelve and the genii* **(Faber)**

This is a gentle fantasy, similar in some ways to *The borrowers* in that it deals with a world scaled down in size. It is based around a set of toy soldiers with which the Brontë children played and invested with lives of their own in the Victorian period. Branwell Brontë wrote down their story in *The history of the young men*. A modern child, Max, finds them under the floorboards, at first a little battered and featureless but soon brought back to life by Max's attention. The complications of their minute existence and the adventures that ensue are told with a careful touch in a story that, though slow moving in places, will appeal to thoughtful readers of a wide variety of ages.

COMMENDED

Gillian Avery. *The greatest Gresham* **(Collins)**

The three Gresham children are very prim and proper while the two Holts are considered totally unsuitable as friends. However, the Holts are determined to broaden the Greshams' horizons and do so in a highly enjoyable romp set in the Victorian period.

Hester Burton. *Castors away!* **(Oxford University Press)**

This fine novel is set at the time of the battle of Trafalgar. A group of children in the Suffolk countryside rescue a soldier escaping arrest. The central character, Nell, stays at home while her brothers leave Suffolk, one to become a surgeon in London, the other to go to sea.

S. E. Ellacott. *Armour and blade* **(Abelard-Schuman)**

This is a very readable history of armoury from the Egyptians to the Second World War. There is a good deal of information included here, much of it told through the use of story.

Penelope Farmer. *The summer birds* **(Chatto & Windus)**

Penelope Farmer is the author of a small number of novels for young adults, all of which are highly regarded by lovers of fantasy. In *The summer birds* Charlotte and Emma meet a boy who teaches each of the children in the village to fly.

Robert Gittings and Jo Manton. *The story of John Keats* **(Methuen)**

Robert Gittings is the author of the standard biographies of the poet. Here he combines with Jo Manton, author of a number of biographies for children, to produce a straightforward account of Keats's life.

K. M. Peyton. *Windfall* **(Oxford University Press)**

Kathleen Peyton's name was one which frequently appeared in the Awards list for the next decade or so. In this novel, an Essex fishing family at the turn of the century saves a man's life. Matt, the rescuer, is rewarded so that his family is able to buy a new fishing boat.

CARNEGIE MEDAL WINNER 1963

Hester Burton. *Time of trial* (Oxford University Press)

The 1960s was a time of recognition for the historical novel and, as has been seen, they figure prominently in the Awards for this period. Like *Castors away!*, Hester Burton's winning novel is set in the Napoleonic period. An old London bookseller, Mr Pargeter, is a follower of Tom Paine's rights of man movement. He publishes a controversial paphlet and is put in prison for sedition. The other theme in the book concerns Margaret, his daughter, who falls in love. This part of the book is beautifully handled and young adults will empathize with it. The atmosphere of London is brought vividly to life in a way that is reminiscent of an historical writer just emerging at this time, Leon Garfield. *Time of trial* is a sensitive portrayal of this period, atmospherically and vividly brought to life.

COMMENDED

Eric Allen. *The latchkey children* (Oxford University Press)

This was considered a very realistic novel in its time and it has continued to be popular since, even though some of its details have dated. Four children meet at a tree after school (they are called latchkey children because their parents are working while they are at home). They discover the tree is to be knocked down and replaced by a concrete engine; their fight to save the tree is brought vividly and accessibly to life.

Ralph Arnold. *Kings, bishops, knights and pawns* (Constable)

This non-fiction title is not about chess as its title might suggest but it is a readable description of feudalism and its importance in medieval society, told in a way which can be understood by children.

Margaret J. Baker. *Castaway Christmas* (Methuen)

Margaret Baker is better known as a fantasy writer. This is a more realistic story dealing with the Ridley family's adventures. They have to cope with floods, danger and near disaster; adult members of the family are conspicuous by their absence.

Antonia Forest. *The Thursday kidnapping* (Faber)

An exciting adventure story which revolves around the four Ramsay children and what happens when a baby in their charge is kidnapped.

John Rowe Townsend. *Hell's edge* (Oxford University Press)

John Rowe Townsend was a powerful force in the development of young adult fiction in Britain. His novels have a gritty realism which still carries some weight today. *Hell's edge* is a good example of his style. Ril hates the new area she has moved to, nicknamed 'Hell's edge'. Her attempts to right the wrongdoing of an ancestor help to bring her together with the community. Two years after this book, Rowe Townsend was to be instrumental in introducing the first serious alternative to the Carnegie Medal, the *Guardian* Award.

CARNEGIE MEDAL WINNER 1964

Sheena Porter. *Nordy Bank* (Oxford University Press)

In the history of the Carnegie Medal only three librarians have won it: Theresa Breslin, Margaret Mahy and (probably the least well known) Sheena Porter. *Nordy Bank* is a very enjoyable example of her work but it is difficult to view it as outstanding. It is a very gentle tale set around the Shropshire hills in which a shy girl, Bron, makes friends with an army dog who has escaped from his handler. The affinity between the two is well defined, as is the sense of atmosphere inspired by the setting. It is very much a 'middle-of-the-road' book: pleasureable to read but not particularly memorable.

COMMENDED

Eric de Mare. *London's river* (Bodley Head)

A well written description of London's River Thames and its history.

J. G. Fyson. *The three brothers of Ur* (Oxford University Press)

This historical novel is concerned with three brothers, sons of a wealthy merchant, who live in the Sumerian city of Ur. Haran, the youngest, breaks out of school and sets off a chain of events by accidentally breaking the image of the Teraphim, the sacred family god. An absorbing but somewhat too literary attempt at recreating an ancient civilization.

C. Walter Hodges. *The namesake* (Bell)

Another historical novel, this time set in King Alfred's time. The narrator, also called Alfred, is assistant to the king's secretary. The enthusiasm of the writer/illustrator, and his description of the Danes and their battles make this an exciting book to read.

K. M. Peyton. *The Maplin Bird* (Oxford University Press)

In this historical novel, Toby and Emily are taken in by their uncle after their parents die in a cholera epidemic. They escape in the boat, the Maplin Bird, in an enjoyable novel whose plotline encompasses smuggling.

CARNEGIE MEDAL WINNER 1965

Philip Turner. *The Grange at High Force* **(Oxford University Press) reissued as** *Adventure at High Force* **J. Goodchild 0 86391 055 6**

It is difficult to separate this book from the swiping criticisms made by Aidan Chambers in his book *The reluctant reader* and from the changes made to the selection committee in the next few years. It was seen that some members of the committee had been there a considerable time and that the same type of book was being honoured each year (and invariably from the same publishing house, Oxford University Press). Philip Turner, a clergyman, had written an enjoyable and often sophisticated book far more likely to appeal to adults than children. The three boy protagonists in the story have cycling adventures on the Yorkshire moors and search for a lost medieval statue. There is also a didactic element in that their quest ends with them also finding God. Chambers felt that this and similar novels 'give a glow of satisfaction when, dressed in their sparkling plastic covers, they line the library shelves, and the publishers' office. There in the main they stay'. With hindsight it is difficult to disagree with that statement.

COMMENDED

J. G. Fyson. *The journey of the eldest son* **(Oxford University Press)**

Another literary work of the period, this is the sequel to *The three brothers of Ur*. Shamashazir wants to accompany one of his father's caravans into the White Mountains but he leaves the city under an evil omen. This is a rite of passage story in that he leaves as a boy but comes back as a man, the future leader of his tribe.

Alan Garner. *Elidor* **(Collins) Collins 0 00 184202 1, 0 00 671674 1; Collins Educational 0 00 330087 0**

Alan Garner was one of the emerging talents in the 1960s as his first two books, *The weirdstone of Brisingamen* and *The moon of Gomrath*, demonstrated. As with those books, *Elidor*'s is a very recognizable, inner city setting which makes the intrusion of magic all the more terrifying. Four Manchester children explore a derelict church and are transported to the world of Elidor which is beset by evil forces. They return with treasures which are in their safe keeping. This is a powerful and original work combining magic and realism in an unusually effective and satisfying way.

Mary K. Harris. *The bus girls* **(Faber)**

A light but readable teenage novel in which 13-year-old Hetty Gray moves to Suffolk and begins an uneasy relationship with Davina, a vicar's daughter, before becoming firm friends with her.

Christopher Headington. *The orchestra and its instruments* **(Bodley Head)**

An absorbing guide to the musical instruments in an orchestra.

K. M. Peyton. *The plan for Bidmarsh* **(Oxford University Press)**

One of this writer's contemporary rather than historical novels, the story concerns a plan to turn Bidmarsh Harbour into a marina which causes Gus no problems but horrifies Paul. He hopes his brother Chris will help stop this plan but Chris is too interested in testing a life-saving suit. An enjoyable piece.

Barbara Leonie Picard. *One is one* **(Oxford University Press)**

This is probably Barbara Leonie Picard's best original work for young people. Stephen wishes to become a knight but his father sends him to a monastery. He runs away from it and is found by Sir Pagan Latourelle who helps him to achieve his ambition.

CARNEGIE MEDAL WINNER 1966

Medal withheld

This outcome caused an enormous amount of controversy. *Junior bookshelf* called it a 'poor, thin way of doing things' and claimed it had 'left everyone concerned feeling rueful and ruffled and looking distinctly shabby'. The presence of Janet Hill, a young and critical librarian, may have affected the committee's decision. Whatever the reason, a Medal has not been withheld since, although selection committees are rumoured sometimes to threaten to withhold as a means of resolving an *impasse*.

HIGHLY COMMENDED

Norman Denny and Josephine Filmer-Sankey. *The Bayeux Tapestry* **(Collins)**

An evocative and stylized account of the events of 1066.

COMMENDED

Helen Griffiths. *The wild horse of Santander* **(Hutchinson)**

This is a horse story written by a highly regarded writer of the genre. A strong relationship develops between the blind Spanish boy Joaquin and his horse Linda. When the boy is taken to hospital for an operation that will help him recover his sight, the horse turns wild.

K. M. Peyton. *Thunder in the sky* **(Oxford University Press)**

Set in 1914, this attractive novel concerns 15-year-old Sam whose elder brother Manny has enlisted. His other brother Gil seems reluctant to do so. There is also concern about the barge Sam works on: is the skipper a spy? The setting echoes the author's later, and more successful, Flambards books (see pp.34 and 35).

Morna Stuart. *Marassa and Midnight* **(Heinemann) Heinemann Educational 0 435 12134 0**

The first multicultural book to appear in the awards lists, it concerns a pair of identical twins. Marassa is bought to become a pageboy in Paris. Midnight runs away from the slave plantation in Haiti to be with his brother. The intervention of two revolutions helps to provide a powerful setting for this historical piece.

CARNEGIE MEDAL WINNER 1967

Alan Garner. *The owl service* **(Collins) Collins 0 00 671675 X, 0 00 674294 7; Collins Educational 0 00 330058 7**

1967 was a classic year as far as British children's literature was concerned, and any of the books on the commended and highly commended lists could be regarded as potential and worthy winners. But Alan Garner's story of a triangular love affair based on a story in the Mabinogion was outstanding even in such a year of quality. Two English children, Roger and Alison, become involved in mysterious events when they hear scratching noises in their loft but all they find there is a dinner service with a design which can be joined together to make the figure of an owl. Their housekeeper's son, Gwyn, is angry at their presence and tension builds up between them and especially between the boys. This results in an abrupt and uncompromising ending. *The owl service* shows Garner at his best and is a powerful and accessible piece of work.

HIGHLY COMMENDED

Henry Treece. *The dream-time* (Brockhampton)

This Award was presented posthumously to a writer who had contributed a number of strongly drawn historical novels but who in this book created something of a more winning standard than in his previous books. The deliberately dream-like quality of the plot tells of a young man at different periods of pre-history who prefers to live in peace with the warring tribes who surround him. *The dream-time* is an unusual but extremely rewarding book whose imagery is matched by the atmospheric illustrations of Charles Keeping who in the same year was the winner of the Kate Greenaway Medal.

COMMENDED

Helen Cresswell. *The piemakers* (Faber)

This is farce of the highest order. The Roller family's livelihood is making pies, with all the members of the family having a role. Arthy, the father, makes the crust, Jem, the mother, grows the herbs while the daughter Gravella deals with the seasonings. Rivalry with other piemakers is rife and when Arthy decides to create a pie for 2000 people in order to enter the Grand Contest, the scene is set for double-crossing of outrageous proportions. *The piemakers* is a witty and very human book which surprises the reader at every turn.

Leon Garfield. *Smith* (Longmans) Puffin 0 14 036458 7, 0 14 038861 3

Garfield had won the *Guardian* Award the previous year for *Devil-in-the-fog* but *Smith* is a much better book. Set in Regency London, with striking images of grime and decadence, it has a particularly appealing hero in the

12-year-old pickpocket, Smith. His adventures begin when he picks the pocket of a man who a few moments later is murdered. Smith has the document which is the reason for the murder but is not pepared to trust anyone for help. An encounter with a blind magistrate (shades of Henry Fielding) makes him question his loyalties and his sense of honour. A hugely enjoyable and deeply moving book which captures the past in a manner which has moved on from the style of those historical novels that were earlier winners of the Medal.

K. M. Peyton. *Flambards* (Oxford University Press) Oxford University Press 0 19 271622 0

As has been seen, Kathleen Peyton's name has appeared frequently in previous commended lists but this and the other books in the Flambards sequence provide writing of a higher order. This, the first part of the sequence, sets the scene in a most dramatic and absorbing way. Christina, a 12-year-old orphan, is sent to live with her crippled uncle in a rambling old house called Flambards. Her uncle's two sons are very different: Mark shares his father's passion for horses while Will is fascinated by aviation. Christina becomes involved with both brothers and with Dick, one of her uncle's employees. Set within the shadows of the First World War, *Flambards* is an absorbing and very readable novel.

CARNEGIE MEDAL WINNER 1968

Rosemary Harris. *The moon in the cloud* (Faber)

In the same year that Ted Hughes's masterpiece *The iron man* was published, the Carnegie selection committee chose to give the Medal to a literary piece set in Biblical times. This is an original book but it is likely to appeal to a small minority of child readers. Set at the time of the Flood, its main characters are not Noah and his family but a young man called Reuben, an animal trainer. He sets off, having been conned by Ham, with a group of talking animals while Ham tries to persuade Thamar, Reuben's wife, that Reuben is dead in order to win her for himself. Reuben does get on the ark but in the guise of the dead Ham. An unusual story.

HONOURS LIST

Joan Aiken. *The whispering mountain* **(Cape) Cape 0 224 61574 2;
Red Fox 0 09 988830 0**

For the next three years the selection committe dispensed with the
Commended and Highly Commended categories and produced an Honours
List, in the manner of the American Newbery Medal. Joan Aiken's novel,
set in the imaginary time of King James III, would no doubt feature in any
such list, whether as commended or with honours. This is one of this fine
writer's most rollicking and wild fantasies. Young Owen's grandfather
finds a legendary golden harp in a ruined monastery. The harp is stolen by
two thieves with their own distinctive line in mock Elizabethan patter and
Owen and his friend Arabis, the daughter of a travelling poet-barber, set
out to find it. All the gothic trappings of such a tale are here (including a
wicked villain, the Marquess of Malyn) in a hugely enjoyable romp which
is very difficult to put down.

Margaret Balderson. *When jays fly to Barbmo* **(Oxford University
Press)**

A thoughtful and quietly written novel about Ingeborg who lives in
German occupied Norway with her father and aunt. After her father's
death, she discovers that her mother was a Lapp and she is forced to
encounter a world different from the farm life she has previously experienced.

Leon Garfield. *Black Jack* **(Longmans) Puffin 0 14 030489 4**

Another of Garfield's powerful historical novels, *Black Jack* is set at the
middle of the eighteenth century. Bartholomew encounters the villanous
Jack and a curious relationship develops between the two of them and the
mad girl, Belle. A dark and often disturbing book which also encompasses
the social injustices of the period.

CARNEGIE MEDAL WINNER 1969

K. M. Peyton. *The edge of the cloud* **(Oxford University Press)
Oxford University Press 0 19 271623 9**

This is the second book in the author's Flambards sequence with all the qualities of the first but heightened so that by the end of the novel the author has achieved something special. Christina is now very firmly involved with Will but he is absorbed by his efforts to fly. This ambition takes him to France where Christina follows him but she misses the rural life of Essex and her horses. The funeral of her hated uncle takes her back to the country but the draw of the aircraft is too much for Will and he pursues his dream in France, with tragic consequences. This is an absorbing book, with the reader becoming easily involved in Will's all-absorbing desire. Christina is an original and sympathetic heroine and the other characters are strongly drawn. However, the choice of *The edge of the cloud* as winner provoked a notorious article in the journal *Children's literature in education* which in turn produced a sharp debate about the book's merits.

HONOURS LIST

Helen Cresswell. *The night-watchmen* (Faber)

Helen Cresswell's work is renowned for its sure comic touch but in this novel she attempts something slightly different and more sinister. Henry stumbles across two tramp-like men, Josh and Caleb, in the park. They interest him with their mysterious talk of 'ticking' and the next time he sees them they are digging a hole with a water pipe at the bottom. But their unexplained reason for doing this and their reference to themselves as night-watchmen intrigues Henry even more. An unusual novel, shot through with the author's humanity and humour.

John Rowe Townsend. *The intruder* (Oxford University Press)

A dark and brooding novel, told with great force by this extremely accomplished writer. Arnold Haithwaite comes upon a mysterious stranger on Skirlston Sands. A somewhat unimaginative 16-year-old, he nevertheless finds something disturbing about the man. When the stranger suggests they might be related, the mystery grows even deeper. A haunting book.

CARNEGIE MEDAL WINNER 1970

Edward Blishen and Leon Garfield. *The god beneath the sea* (Longman)

Leon Garfield's name had appeared a number of times in the commended categories of the Award but his only time as winner was as joint author of this collection of Greek myths and legends. These are powerful and uncompromising versions of the stories, told without any Victorian affectation but with a muscular modern feel. The narrative is continuous, with the stories flowing on from each other. The first part of the book is concerned with the creation of the gods, the second with the making of men by Prometheus against the wishes of Zeus and, with the creation of Pandora, the third part describes how gods and men intermingled and fought against each other. More than with most Carnegie winners, it is difficult to divorce the strength of the writing from Charles Keeping's powerfully dramatic illustrations which appeared in the Kate Greenaway medals list in the same year. Despite its obvious merits, *The god beneath the sea* began the debate which was to continue over the next decade and to culminate with the Medal winners being described as 'the great unread'. It was felt by a significant number of librarians that although the book was good, it was not read primarily by children. Obviously a book of Greek myths is not going to be popular with everyone but that should not deter readers from attempting it.

HONOURS LIST

Peter Dickinson. *The devil's children* (Gollancz)

This was the first appearance on the list of Peter Dickinson, who later won the Carnegie Medal twice. *The devil's children* is the third book in a sequence known as 'The changes' because it takes place during a five-year period when the English world has turned against machinery and other aspects of modern civilization. The devil's children is the name given to a group of Sikhs with whom Nicky takes refuge. They are reluctant to take her in but realize she is as important to their survival as they are to her. The book is also a plea for tolerance as the Sikhs are regarded with suspicion when they finally do settle into their new surroundings.

Leon Garfield. *The drummer boy* (Longman)

This is Garfield in his more typical historical mode. A dark and powerful work, it centres on the disillusionment of the drummer boy, Charlie, who has set off with high hopes for the war with France, only to return to England driven by the terror of a ghost from the battlefield pursuing him. The intervention and love of Charity, a general's daughter, helps to bring Charlie peace but only after a number of disturbing episodes, described with vivid candour.

William Mayne. *Ravensgill* (Hamish Hamilton)

In another of this writer's absorbing works, Bob White and Judith Chapman have to contend with their two families being at war. They attempt to unravel the mystery of how the feud began and find it centres around Bob's grandmother harbouring a murderer at Ravensgill. A powerfully written and approachable book.

CARNEGIE MEDAL WINNER 1971

Ivan Southall. *Josh* (Angus and Robertson)

It was stated from the from the inception of the Carnegie Medal that winners should be members of the British Empire who wrote in English and whose books were first published in the United Kingdom. However, in 1969 the terms of the Award were changed so that books by writers of any nationality were eligible as long as they were published simultaneously in Britain and their country of origin. It was therefore almost inevitable that an Australian should be the first non-UK resident to win the Medal. Ivan Southall had a reputation at the time of writing of strongly drawn characters in realistic settings. *Josh* is set in the 1930s but the feelings described in it could happen at any time or in any place. Josh is fourteen and has to travel from his urban home to stay with his Aunt Clara in the outback. The trip is a disaster from the beginning and when Josh finally arrives, he is dismayed by the apparent poverty of his aunt's surroundings and by the village where she lives. He is regarded as an outsider by the villagers and the children do their best to match his truculence with theirs. Josh achieves a kind of peace with them and the rest of the village, but only after he has decided to leave. This is an unusual and cleverly constructed novel, dealing with tolerance and with a teenage boy's right to be honest about his feelings.

HIGHLY COMMENDED

Gillian Avery. *A likely lad* (Collins)

Another of Gillian Avery's highly polished comedies of manners, placed in her beloved Victorian England. Set in Manchester, it has a winning hero in Willy Overs, a timid and bookish boy whose father has ambitions for him to 'get on'. Willy discovers he has an aunt whose existence has been kept from him and her unconventional ways help him to defy his father and make his escape when he is thwarted from staying on at school. A light and comic tale with a cast of strongly drawn characters.

Helen Cresswell. *Up the pier* (Faber)

This well-written and moving novel is the story of Carrie and the mysterious family, the Pontifexes, who arrive on the pier after a time travel from 1921. Carrie has to find a way to release them from the forces on either side of the pier which have trapped them in the middle. The loneliness and dreariness of a seaside town out of season are well captured, as are the various characters, particularly those who are evil.

Rosemary Sutcliff. *Tristan and Iseult* (Bodley Head) Heinemann Educational 0 435 12177 4

This is a superb retelling of the famous legend. Tristan gets Iseult for his uncle King Mark but realizes that he loves her himself. Set in the Celtic world of Ireland, Cornwall and Brittany, this is a masterly version which brings the past immediately and vibrantly to life.

CARNEGIE MEDAL WINNER 1972

Richard Adams. *Watership Down* (Rex Collings) Penguin 0 14 003958 9; Puffin 0 14 030601 3, 0 14 036453 6; Viking 0 670 85165 5

The story behind the publication of this epic novel is now legendary. Rejected by most publishers partly because of its length and partly because of the references to classical writers mixed in with the story, it was finally published by a small independent publisher. It then went on to become a huge international success, winning both the Carnegie Medal and the *Guardian* Award, and has been filmed. It is one of the few children's books to appear both on a children's and an adult's publishing list, adding to the debate about whether Carnegie Medal winners were really read by children although it is indisputable that a wide variety of young people read and enjoy it. It is an animal story with human beings restricted very much to the sidelines, in which a warren of rabbits is warned by the prophetic Fiver of impending doom and disaster; only a small number of them follow him to find a new home. His brother Hazel reluctantly takes on the role of leader. As they travel, they tell each other stories of the ways of rabbits, most notably through the legendary rabbit figure of El-ahrairah. Realizing that without any females the tribe will die, they set off in search of some, only to encounter the strict regime of General Woundwort. The reader becomes totally involved in their quest and wills them to succeed. *Watership Down* is a novel that defies classification, although it follows a tradition of animal fantasy. Its epic scale can be daunting but it is difficult not to become involved in the plot and to sympathize with the characters.

COMMENDED

Peter Dickinson. *The dancing bear* (Gollancz)

Set in sixth century Byzantium, Dickinson's enthralling novel tells the story of three beings, all born on the same day: Bubba the dancing bear, Silvester the slave who cares for her and Ariadne whose father owns Silvester. When the Huns raid the city, Ariadne is captured and Silvester and the bear set off in search of her. The sights and smells of the period are vividly brought to life in a skilfully drawn portrait of a period unknown to most readers.

Emma Smith. *No way of telling* (Bodley Head)

Amy and her grandmother live in an isolated Welsh Cottage. When snow arrives, they are housebound but the snow also brings with it a stranger and four days of terror. A gripping book with a telling depiction of a rural life which is not as idyllic as that usually portrayed in books for young people.

CARNEGIE MEDAL WINNER 1973

Penelope Lively. *The ghost of Thomas Kempe* (Heinemann)
Heinemann Educational 0 435 12204 5; Mammoth 0 7497 0791 7

There was criticism for some time that Carnegie Medal winners were not read by children. Whether by coincidence or not, the winners over the next decade were in the main those which were not only highly praised by adults but were also enjoyed by many young readers. Penelope Lively's novel has the appeal of a ghost story, although one with a light touch, but the author also brings to it an assured touch gained through the authorship of a number of polished previous books. The Harrison family move into a cottage not knowing that the spirit of a seventeenth century sorcerer, Thomas Kempe, has been released during the cottage's renovation.

James, the son, suspects something is wrong when things go missing and he finds notes written in archaic language. Kempe soon makes his presence felt and shows his horror at twentieth-century life, offering suggestions as to how its problems can be solved by sorcery. Although the story is told with a light touch, potential tragedy looms when Kempe accuses a villager of being a witch and sets fire to her cottage. The juxtaposition of the reality of village life and the supernatural conjurings of a cantankerous seventeenth-century sorcerer makes for a winning formula still greatly enjoyed by a large number of young readers.

COMMENDED

Nina Bawden. *Carrie's war* (Gollancz) Hamish Hamilton 0 241 13544 3; Heinemann Educational 0 435 12202 9; Puffin 0 14 030689 7, 0 14 036456 0

Nina Bawden is one of the most skilled writers for children of the latter half of the twentieth century. Her books are both approachable for young readers and of a high enough literary standard to satisfy adult critics. *Carrie's war* is one of her very best. Partly based on the author's own feelings as an evacuee, it takes place during the Second World War. Carrie and her brother Nick are evacuated to Wales to live with the miserly Mr Evans and his sister Auntie Lou. Their friend Albert is in much better surroundings, staying with the exotic Hepzibah and strange Mr Johnny at Druids Bottom. The dramatic events that occur through Carrie's intervention provide a contrast with the domestic boredom of much of the village's lives and the moving climax brings the book up to the present day.

Susan Cooper. *The dark is rising* (Chatto & Windus) Bodley Head 0 370 30815 8; Puffin 0 14 030799 0, 0 14 036462 5

This is the second in a sequence of five fantasy novels which is known by the title of this particular book. Will awakes on Midwinter Day, the morning of his eleventh birthday, to a waiting world outside his own time. He has to find and join together the five remaining signs of the light and only he, the last born of the Old Ones, has the power to accomplish this task. This is a highly atmospheric and powerful book in which Will, as representative of the Forces of Light, has to prevent the Dark from rising.

Helen Cresswell. *The bongleweed* **(Faber)**

Another splendid novel from this highly creative writer. Becky's parents, Else and Finch, have a passion for gardening so when a flowering plant begins to spread all over their neighbourhood they are delighted. However, the bongleweed, as Becky christens it, seems to be spreading all over England. It is then that Becky decides to take action. Helen Cresswell's characterization again comes to the fore in this very readable book.

CARNEGIE MEDAL WINNER 1974

Mollie Hunter. *The stronghold* **(Hamish Hamilton) Canongate 0 86241 500 4**

Historical fiction had not figured strongly in the Medal winners for some time, perhaps reflecting its general wane in popularity. The setting for this novel is Scotland in the first century AD. Coll, foster son of his tribe's chief, tries to persuade the rest of the tribe to provide a stronghold in order to help prevent invasion by the Romans. The boy was crippled by an attacking troop when younger and his father was killed. The rest of the tribe is divided between the views of Nectan who believes they should retreat out of sight when attacked and Domnall, the high priest, who wants them to stay and fight. Coll's stronghold tower is seen as a compromise. The appearance of a stranger, Taran, disrupts the plan even more. This is a powerful book with descriptions which do not disguise the violence of the times. It was the first book by a Scottish writer to be awarded the Medal but its Orkney setting may limit its readership. It was awarded in a year when a new type of Medal was introduced in Britain, the Other Award, intended to highlight books which promoted non-stereotypical situations.

HIGHLY COMMENDED

Ian Ribbons. *The Battle of Gettysburg* **(Oxford University Press)**

This is a highly illustrated non-fiction title depicting the story of the three day-long battle in the American Civil War.

COMMENDED

Winifred Cawley. *Gran at Coalgate* **(Oxford University Press)**

A warm-hearted story set in 1920s Northumberland. Jinnie is becoming anxious about her forthcoming scholarship exam so her doctor prescribes a break. She is sent to stay with her grandmother in the mining community of Coalgate. She has inherited the intolerant attitudes of her father so it is quite a shock to discover her grandmother is far more liberal than she is. Set against the background of Britain's General Strike, this is a compassionate novel about a girl taking her first steps towards independent thinking.

Jill Paton Walsh. *The Emperor's winding sheet* **(Macmillan)**

Jill Paton Walsh has made such a significant contribution to children's literature that it is perhaps surprising to discover that this is her only appearance on the Carnegie list. Winner of the Whitbread Award, *The emperor's winding sheet* tells the story of the fall of Constantinople. A boy accidentally falls out of a tree at the feet of the last Emperor of the Romans. The subject of this book, how this event transforms his life and how the relationship between the two develops, is captured in subtle prose and with a sympathetic feeling for the period.

CARNEGIE MEDAL WINNER 1975

Robert Westall. *The machine gunners* **(Macmillan) Heinemann Educational 0 435 12457 9; Piper 0 330 33428 X**

This was the first work by a prolific writer whose work was to figure prominently in the later years of the Award, both as winner and in the commended categories. *The machine gunners* is a fresh and hugely enjoyable novel, set in Tyneside during the Second World War. Chas McGill has a collection of war souvenirs and he and his gang often go in search of debris dropped by bombers. He finds a crashed German plane and manages to wrench free the machine gun which he and his friends intend to use to protect their country. Unfortunately the one German to survive the crash is not the monster propaganda has led them to expect but a gentle pilot, Rudi. Their efforts to conceal the gun and the pilot lead them into deeper trouble. This is a strong and vivid book, told directly and with some swearing, and with some strong characters, including the local bully Boddser Brown who has the best collection of war souvenirs in town. The setting and storyline make it a book which strongly appeals to boys although it did not receive universal approval as winner. Eight children's librarians from the London Borough of Bromley complained about its violence and bad language, asking 'isn't it about time that the Medal was again awarded to a real children's book as it was originally intended?' Westall's own comments about what happened to him as a writer after winning the Medal are vividly described in an article he wrote for the journal *Signal*, 28, January 1979.

COMMENDED

Susan Cooper. *The grey king* **(Chatto & Windus) Bodley Head 0 370 30828 X; Puffin 0 14 030952 7**

The fourth in the Dark is Rising sequence (see p.41), this book has the unique distinction of being the only one to appear on the Carnegie Medal list and to be awarded the American Newbery Medal. This was because a system had been introduced whereby a book published in another country within six months of its UK publication would be eligible for the Medal. Susan Cooper's book continued her powerful and dramatic series. Will's quest is to wake the six sleepers from the hill and to make them ready for the last battle between the dark and the light. This continues a legend that in a hill in Wales lies a harp of gold which will be found by a boy and a white dog with silver eyes.

Diana Wynne Jones. *Dogsbody* **(Macmillan) Mammoth 0 7497 1260 0**

Diana Wynne Jones is a fantasy writer whose quirky books are highly regarded by many and enjoyed by young people. The Luminaries have made judgement on Sirius the Dog-Star that he be forced to remain as a dog in an earthly household while searching for the Zoi, a mysterious murder weapon. Sirius's owner is Kathleen who has a father in the Maze prison and a family which hates dogs. How Sirius survives under the circumstances and attempts to find the Zoi is told in a deftly judged comic manner but one which has serious undertones.

CARNEGIE MEDAL WINNER 1976

Jan Mark. *Thunder and Lightnings* **(Kestrel) Puffin 0 14 031063 0, 0 14 036617 2**

This is the first book of a writer who has since gone on to make a significant contribution to children's literature. It was in fact the winner of a competition jointly organized by Penguin and *The Guardian*; it went on to win the *Guardian* Award as well as the Carnegie Medal. It is a deliciously fresh story about Andrew, who has recently moved to Norfolk. He makes friends with Victor, a highly individual boy, whose home life is presented in stark contrast to Andrew's more bohemian family life. Victor is not an achiever in school with his highly original attempts at spelling, but he has a passion for aeroplanes and knows everything about the Lightnings that are made not far from the village. However, Andrew discovers that the factory is to be replaced by one making Jaguars. *Thunder and Lightnings* is a book shot through with Jan Mark's perceptive observation and, in its depiction of everyday life, manages to be both rich and colourful.

COMMENDED

Peter Dickinson. *The blue hawk* (Gollancz)

This is one of Dickinson's historical books which seem to find greater favour with the selection committee than his books with a more modern setting. Tron is the only person who can tame the hawk sufficiently to sit on his wrist. From the first time he touches the bird, he seems to be able to control the actions of his nation. He is able to hear the words of the Gods and to carry out their desires in order to save his nation. This is an imaginative and powerful novel, set in a time that could equally be one of the ancient civilizations or set sometime in the future.

CARNEGIE MEDAL WINNER 1977

Gene Kemp. *The turbulent term of Tyke Tiler* (Faber) Collins Educational 0 00 330021 8; Puffin 0 14 031135 1, 0 14 036610 5

It is difficult to describe this book without giving away the secret of its sting in the tail. This is so cleverly done that most readers are completely taken by surprise and are tempted to re-read the book to find out where their assumptions went wrong. Its cheeky, slapstick style was not popular with everyone at the time particularly with some adult critics, and even with a few members of the selection panel, but it has been continually popular with younger readers ever since publication. Tyke is always trying to compensate for the failures of Danny Price who is endearing but not too bright and whose escapades are threatening to blight his future at Cricklepit Combined School. This results in the possibility of his being sent to a school for children with learning difficulties until Tyke finds the test papers for the school on the headteacher's desk and is tempted. This is a witty and hugely enjoyable romp obviously geared towards the age group which the Carnegie Medal, with its increasing emphasis on teenage fiction, was being accused of avoiding.

COMMENDED

Peter Carter. *Under Goliath* (Oxford University Press) Nelson 0 17 432298 4; Puffin 0 14 031132 7

Peter Carter is the author of a number of powerfully written novels. This one is set in Ulster in 1969. Alan and his family live under the shadow of Goliath, the giant crane which dominates the landscape. He joins an Orange Band, not particularly for any sectarian reason but because he loves playing music. However, the bitterness of divided communities in Northern Ireland soon begin to impinge upon his life. A strong and provocative novel with a setting rare in young people's literature.

Diana Wynne Jones. *Charmed life* (Macmillan) Mammoth 0 7497 1473 5

This is a light and frothy fantasy, told with great skill and style. Gwendolen has obvious gifts as a witch but her brother Cat sometimes feels that she makes too much of her gifts. When the two are whisked away to Chrestomanci Castle by the mysterious Chrestomanci himself there are even more concerns as Gwendolen's powers are put into doubt by the great man himself. Cat begins to feel that she will have to try even more outrageous tricks to try to convince the enchanter that she does have outstanding talents.

Philippa Pearce. *The shadow-cage* (Kestrel) Puffin 0 14 031073 8

This is a collection of ten supernatural stories by one of the best technicians in children's writing. The mysterious events take place in real surroundings which makes them all the more disturbing, such as the small bottle in the title story. Each of the three people who handle it recognizes its full power but only Kevin is caught in the full power of the bottle's attraction. It is always difficult to assess a collection like this in the same way as a novel as some stories are often weaker than others but *The shadow-cage* contains stories of equal power.

CARNEGIE MEDAL WINNER 1978

David Rees. *The Exeter blitz* **(Hamish Hamilton)**

David Rees was the writer of a number of interesting and approachable works as well as of criticism of other children's writers. In the 1980s he began to write mainly for adults although his controversial novel about gay teenagers, *The milkman's on his way* is still read by both adults and young people. It is probably unfortunate that the selection committee chose to honour *The Exeter blitz* for it is not one of his strongest works. As its title suggests, it is set in the Second World War. Colin Lockwood watches the bombing of Exeter from the cathedral tower on the night of 3–4 May 1942. Although he enjoys the excitement of the raid, he begins to become concerned about the rest of the family and goes in search of them. A gentle and quiet book, this is an enjoyable read although it has been criticized for tampering with historical fact. This will not deter young people who may well get some pleasure from the story.

COMMENDED

Bernard Ashley. *A kind of wild justice* **(Oxford University Press)**
Oxford University Press 0 19 271617 4

Bernard Ashley, then a London headteacher, is renowned for his gritty and unsentimental portrayals of working-class life. *A kind of wild justice* takes place in London's East End and revolves around the activities of the Bradshaw brothers, criminals whose activities impinge upon much of the community. Ronnie's father has become caught up in their affairs and Ronnie is terrified of what they might do to his family. His fear becomes so obsessional that he has to do something about it. Unfortunately his actions have a dire effect upon the life of Manjit, his school friend. Ashley tackles themes like racism and violence in a non-judgmental way which helps young readers to come to terms with the life that exists in the novel.

Philippa Pearce. *The battle of Bubble and Squeak* **(Andre**
Deutsch) Andre Deutsch 0 233 96986 1; Puffin 0 14 031183 1

Philippa Pearce's name appears yet again on the list for a book which also won the Whitbread Award. The scene is domestic and though the book's subject matter may appear minor, to the children in the story it is highly important as it probably would be to most child readers. Bubble and Squeak are two gerbils, acquired by the three Parker children much against their mother's will. She hates animals and fights against Sid, Peggy and Amy who want to keep them. Their mild-mannered stepfather, who owned white mice as a boy, reluctantly becomes part of the battle. All this is tellingly told in a deceptively simple way which will appeal to young readers, many of whom may well have encountered a similar situation.

Robert Westall. *The devil on the road* **(Macmillan) Pan 0 330 34064 6**

This is a powerful time-slip story. John Webster is a biker who enjoys roaming the countryside. One night he stays in the barn of a couple who are very eager for him to stay. His only companion in the barn is a mysterious cat which appears to be able to get in and out without passing through the door. John gets involved in the violent affairs of the Puritan era, all the time believing that the actions he follows are his own choice. Westall cleverly plays with the reader's perceptions as his protagonist becomes further involved in events which will inevitably carry on around him.

CARNEGIE MEDAL WINNER 1979

Peter Dickinson. *Tulku* **(Gollancz) Corgi 0 552 52812 9**

This fine historical novel was also the winner of the Whitbread Award and is set during a period not familiar to many readers, the Boxer Rebellion in China. Theodore is the only survivor of an attack on his father's mission settlement. He escapes and meets up with the larger than life Mrs Jones, an ageing botanist. Together they head for the forbidden territory of Tibet. There they find refuge in the monastery of Dong Pe although Theodore feels that something other than chance is bringing them there. The old Lama is convinced that they hold the clue to the birth of the Tulku, a priestly saviour, but the boy has to wrestle with the entrenched attitudes of his Christian upbringing before he can consider helping the monks. This is an exciting and strongly written novel, with a powerful motif concerning religions and the right to live one's own life. Mrs Jones has certainly done that and in her risqué attitude Dickinson has created one of his most appealing and attractive characters. She carries the story forward but at its heart is Theodore, who is forced to challenge the beliefs that have been handed down to him from childhood.

HIGHLY COMMENDED

Sheila Sancha. *The castle story* (Kestrel)

The highly commended category, a regular feature of the awards from this period, has continued to the present day. This book is unusual in its presentation with an approachable and enjoyable text. It tells the story of a castle and is interesting in the way it mingles past depictions of the castle with modern cartoons.

COMMENDED

Eva Ibbotson. *Which witch?* (Macmillan) Pan 0 330 26586 5

This is farce of the highest order. Eva Ibbotson has written a number of funny novels involving magic and this is probably her best. Arriman the Awful, the local Great Wizard, is becoming bored with his job and wants someone new to take over. He decides the only way to achieve this is to marry. Because he has to marry a witch and because the local selection disgusts him, he decides to hold a contest in which the witch who does the foulest deed will get his hand. Belladonna, a white witch, wants to enter but her profession despises dark deeds. However, with some help, she does. A light and frothy work.

Ann Schlee. *The vandal* (Macmillan)

In contrast, Ann Schlee's futuristic novel, which also won the *Guardian* Award, could not be grimmer. It takes place on the Estates, where people are conditioned to forget their past deeds and to accept no responsibility for them. Paul is branded a vandal because he starts fires but he wants to remember what he has done and why he has done it. An encounter with an unconventional family, the Willmays, makes him challenge his psychiatrist and ultimately the system, a challenge which brings him into great danger. This is a powerful and believeable novel which will have some appeal to young adults.

CARNEGIE MEDAL WINNER 1980

Peter Dickinson. *City of gold* (Gollancz) Hamish Hamilton 0 241 13920 1

Peter Dickinson was the first writer to win the Medal in successive years but this year's Award was for a very different book from *Tulku*. This is a collection of Bible stories, retold in strong and often gritty prose. Thirty-three stories from the pre-Exile period are recounted in a distinctive and sometimes unusual way. For example, the story of David and Goliath is recounted by an army sergeant as a good example of tactical manoeuvres. It is a splendid example of how familiar stories can be brought to life by a writer at the height of his powers. However, it was not a particularly popular choice and added fuel to the argument that the Medal was being awarded to books which failed to find a child audience. One correspondent to *Library Association record* wrote 'as regards the Award in general, why does the committee so often choose something no "ordinary" child will read?'

HIGHLY COMMENDED

Jan Mark. *Nothing to be afraid of* (Kestrel) Puffin 0 14 031392 3

This is a collection of short stories, set in the 1950s. Each of the ten stories takes an everyday event and gives it a twist which makes the reader slightly uneasy. For example, William tells his granny the story of 'The three little pigs' but in a version radically different from the original. There is Brenda, trapped in the middle of animosity between her teachers, and Arthur who thinks he knows everything. Often the sinister aspects of the stories are hinted at rather than made explicit, as in the possibility of a ghost, which adds a *frisson*. This is a macabre and often humorous collection of stories.

COMMENDED

John Branfield. *The fox in winter* (Gollancz) Collins 0 00 330000 5

This teenage novel has an unusual subject: the friendship that develops between an adolescent girl and an old man. Fran's mother, Nancy, is a district nurse and the girl finds herself becoming more attached to 90-year-old Tom Treloar, one of her mother's patients. He is determined that, despite family pressure, he and his wife Lettie will stay in the home where they have lived all their lives. Unfortunately Lettie has to be admitted to hospital and, after her death, Tom stays on in the house, where he relies more and more upon Fran, with whom he shares the events of his life. This is a successfully drawn portrait of the extremes of youth and age sharing a life together, with a moving ending.

Jan Needle. *A sense of shame* **(Andre Deutsch)**

The second collection of short stories to appear in this year's list, *A sense of shame* is another book for teenagers. Jan Needle was one of the writers emerging during this period who was prepared to look at aspects of modern life such as racism. Each of the seven stories examines an aspect of prejudice. The story from which the collection takes its name, for example, deals with the relationship that develops between a Pakistani boy and a white Catholic girl. Mohammed and Lorraine share a glorious summer together but she knows that the relationship is doomed to fail. A powerful but uneven collection.

CARNEGIE MEDAL WINNER 1981

Robert Westall. *The scarecrows* **(Chatto & Windus) Heinemann Educational 0 435 12289 4; Puffin 0 14 037308 X**

Westall's second Medal winner caused a good deal of controversy. It is an uncompromising book definitely intended for young adults. Simon is unhappy that his mother has married Joe Moreton, a man very different from his real father, a man who had died for the British Army. He takes to spending much of his time at the old deserted water mill where sometimes he can hear noises of ghostly footsteps. When two scarecrows appear in the field by the mill, the scene is set for a dramatic confrontation between Simon and his pacifist stepfather. The power of the descriptions and the scene where Simon voyeuristically watches his mother and stepfather making love caused a certain amount of concern. An anonymous writer in *Times educational supplement* commented on this and the year's Kate Greenaway Medal winner, *The highwayman*, 'a modicum of blood and damage are needed these days to twitch the little ones into a happier understanding of the world they live in' and continued with some disparaging remarks about *The scarecrows*. This provoked an angry response from Westall when he collected his Medal at the annual conference.

HIGHLY COMMENDED

Jane Gardam. *The hollow land* **(Julia MacRae) Walker 0 7445 2372 9**

This is a collection of stories about life in the countryside by a writer as famous for her adult novels. Set in Cumbria, the stories have a common theme: the difference between those who have lived in the country for generations and the 'incomers' who move from the towns and cities into second homes. The characterization ranges from Bell and Harry, who are friends for life, to the haunting tale of the Egg Witch and her mother. The longer final story is set in the future. This is a satisfying and highly accomplished collection that will provide young people from any background with a good deal of food for thought.

COMMENDED

Jane Gardam. *Bridget and William* (Julia MacRae)

The same writer provides a less ambitious but still highly enjoyable and satisfying read. It demonstrates how in a relatively brief text (it was published in a series designed for fledgling readers) the depths of human emotions can be portrayed. Bridget's father dislikes her pony, William, but the animal proves he is worth his weight in gold after the night of the great snow storm. In simple and highly effective prose, Jane Gardam can capture a feeling in a few brief sentences.

Michelle Magorian. *Goodnight Mister Tom* (Kestrel) Puffin 0 14 031541 1, 0 14 037233 4

This book caused an enormous sensation when it was first published and it continues to capture the hearts of new generations of readers. Set in 1939, it tells how the timid evacuee, Willie Beech, transforms the life of the widower Tom Oakley whose wife and child had died 40 years previously. Willie gains in confidence, spurred on by his fellow evacuee Zach. However, he is summoned back to London by his mother, a guilt-ridden religious psychopath. After a series of harrowing encounters, he is rescued by Tom. This is a deeply emotional roller coaster of a book which appeals to a wide age range of readers.

CARNEGIE MEDAL WINNER 1982

Margaret Mahy. *The haunting* (Dent) Dent 0 460 06097 X; Heinemann Educational 0 435 12286 X; Puffin 0 14 036325 4

This was the first of two books with a supernatural theme written by this versatile author, the first from New Zealand to be awarded the Medal. Barney realizes he is to be invaded by the ghost of his Great-Uncle Cole but the rest of his immediate family is sceptical about the haunting. However, relatives of his dead mother recognize that he has unusual powers. His sister Tabitha, a very practical girl, decides to find out the truth behind the haunting but in the end it is one of their brothers, Troy, who makes the final connection. As is to be expected from a writer of Mahy's calibre, this is no ordinary ghost story. The events help to disturb tensions within the family but in the end this strengthen the bonds between the very different family members. The writer's prose glistens like polished metal, clever and urbane while also being approachable. It is a book whose nuances young readers may fail to notice, but one which they can hardly fail to appreciate.

HIGHLY COMMENDED

Gillian Cross. *The dark behind the curtain* (Oxford University Press)

This was the first of this fine writer's mature works. In some ways it resembles *The haunting* in that at one level it can be read as a ghost story but it also provides food for thought about issues such as loyalty. The plot revolves around a school production of the Victorian melodrama *Sweeney Todd*. Two boys, both called Colin, are involved: they have known each other since childhood. Colin Marshall has the role of Sweeney but it seems to bring out his innate nastiness. As Colin Jackus discovers, the play disturbs the spirits of Victorian poorhouse children. Ann Ridley, also an outsider, works with Jackus to decipher the mystery. This has enough cleverly written sequences to produce shivers down the spine but it also raises issues which the young reader can take on board, perhaps even without realizing how it is done.

COMMENDED

Tim Kennemore. *Wall of words* (Faber)

Tim Kennemore bursts upon the children's literature world with a prolific number of novels. She is a writer of skill and ingenuity, able to produce work in a variety of genres. This is a family story. Mr Tate, the father of four daughters, has left home to write a novel, and the children and their mother are left to carry on as best they can. The eldest daughter, Kim, is determined to find him but concerns are expressed about Kerry who has problems at school. How Kerry resolves these problems and how the rest of the family copes with the situation is delightfully told in an enjoyable and witty book.

CARNEGIE MEDAL WINNER 1983

Jan Mark. *Handles* (Kestrel) Puffin 0 14 031587 X

This is domestic comedy at the highest level. Erica is a motor-cycle buff who is looking forward to spending her summer holidays with the rest of her gang, hanging around in the city where she lives. Unfortunately her mother has other ideas and sends her to live with her aunt and uncle and their terrible son Robert in the country. This family is described by Jan Mark with satisfyingly wicked cruelty as probably the most boring collection of people in the world. Erica chances upon a nearby town, Polthorpe, which boasts Britain's smallest industrial estate and there she encounters as eccentric a set of characters, including Bill Birdcycle and the Gremlin, as even she could hope for. This was Jan Mark's second Medal winner and in its own quiet way it asks as many questions as some more portentous novels. It also benefits from the writer's skill in capturing a situation with a pithy and unforgettable *bon mot*.

HIGHLY COMMENDED

James Watson. *Talking in whispers* (Gollancz) Collins Educational 0 00 330028 5; Armada 0 00 672378 0

This powerful novel is set in Chile, 'sometime between the present and the future', although a reader with a rudimentary knowledge of South American history will recognize some of the situations. Andres, son of an anti-establishment singer, escapes when his father's car is ambushed. He is helped by a brother and sister, twin puppeteers. The main political opponent of the Junta is also shot prior to an election which would put him in power, and Andres receives the photographic evidence which shows a member of the Secret Service carrying out the shooting. How Andres helps to bring the truth to the world is told in an exciting and absorbing way. There are some terrifying scenes such as the one where Andres is tortured but *Talking in whispers* is a compassionate and powerful book.

COMMENDED

Philippa Pearce. *The way to Sattin Shore* (Kestrel) Puffin 0 14 031644 2

Eagerly awaited, this was Philippa Pearce's first full-length novel for some years. In the event it turned out to be a curious mixture of a book albeit with some powerful passages. Kate has always assumed she is fatherless until her father's gravestone disappears. Her family obviously has some secret to hide but in the meantime Kate's life continues as normal. She enjoys the company of her cat, Syrup, makes a new friend at school and has adventures with her two older brothers. But all these adventures take her back to Sattin Shore where her father is supposed to have drowned and where one day a naked man emerges from the water.

Patricia Wrightson. *A little fear* **(Hutchinson) Hutchinson 0 09 152710 4**

This Australian novel introduces two personable characters: old Mrs Tucker who does not want to leave her isolated cottage, and the Njimbin, an ancient creature with whom she fights over the land. The old lady does not want to exchange her home for a room in an old people's home but when the Njimbin is provoked by gunshots he begins to set in motion a course of events during which Mrs Tucker begins to doubt her sanity. The book is all the more terrifying because everyday things suddenly turn on the old woman and there is a satisfyingly creepy feel about the powerfully told events.

CARNEGIE MEDAL WINNER 1984

Margaret Mahy. *The changeover* **(Dent) Puffin 0 14 037295 4**

Warned by a voice inside her head that something terrible is about to happen, Laura is helpless to do anything about it. The evil Carmody Braque begins to prey on Jacko, her younger brother, and is able to suck the life-force from him. Laura is the only one who can save him but to do so she will have to make use of her own latent supernatural powers. This means reaching out to Sorrel Carlisle and his family and a blossoming relationship between the two develops. This is both a realistic novel about changing family patterns involving teenagers and a most credible fantasy: the scene where Carmody stamps the boy's hand in order to begin draining his life force is truly terrifying. *The changeover* further demonstrates Margaret Mahy's skill in whatever style she uses.

HIGHLY COMMENDED

Robert Swindells. *Brother in the land* **(Oxford University Press)**
Oxford University Press 0 19 271552 6; Puffin 0 14 037300 4

This is a gripping novel set in Britain after a nuclear holocaust. Written
through the eyes of Danny, one of the few survivors of an attack on an ordinary town, it graphically describes the effects of nuclear war. Although
Swindells does not shirk from describing horrific sights and bestial behaviour, this is not a sensationalist book but a deeply committed look at probable events. Danny has to cope with defending his father's shop from
looters and with looking after his younger brother, Ben. They befriend a
girl, Kim, and set off in search of a better life. There is some optimism that
the human spirit will continue but Swindells pulls no punches in letting
his young adult audience know how bleak life would be in such circumstances. The author made a very moving speech when he accepted the commendation, saying that he had always wanted to have a Highly
Commended nomination since his hero, Henry Treece, received one.

CARNEGIE MEDAL WINNER 1985

Kevin Crossley-Holland. *Storm* **(Heinemann) Heinemann 0 434
93032 6**

There has always been criticism that the winners of the Medal are invariably books intended for teenagers. This is almost inevitable because, in
books of such length, the author has space to expand upon plot and characterization and the other features that are important criteria for awards.
It was therefore with some relief that the selection committee was able to
make what was described in some circles as a brave choice in presenting
the Medal to a short book in a series for new readers. On a wild stormy
night Annie is offered a ride by a tall, silent horseman. She overcomes her
fear of the ghost who is said to haunt the lonely road and accepts the ride.
But as the journey progresses so does her trepidation: just who is this mysterious stranger? All this is told with a poet's skill and a number of felici-
tous touches. The descriptions of the dramatic journey are powerfully done
and in no way could the work be described as formula writing, as often happens with titles in series such as the one in which *Storm* is published.

HIGHLY COMMENDED

Janni Howker. *The nature of the beast* **(Julia MacRae)**
Heinemann Educational 0 435 12459 5; Walker 0 7445 4350 9

Janni Howker burst upon the children's book world with a superb collection of short stories, *Badger on the barge*, which inexplicably was not on the Carnegie winners' list. This gritty and uncompromising book set in a Northern town gripped by high unemployment was her first novel. Sheep farmers say there is a killer dog on the loose but local children think it must be a monster. Young Bill Coward reckons he's seen the beast and is determined to track it down, despite the apathy of a community too devastated by the loss of jobs to care. The development of the novel in making the reader doubt the existence of a beast until the gripping climax is achieved with enormous artistry. The book was the recipient of other awards such as the *Young Observer* Teenage Fiction Prize and the Whitbread Award.

CARNEGIE MEDAL WINNER 1986

Berlie Doherty. *Granny was a buffer girl* **(Methuen) Heinemann**
Educational 0 435 12328 9; Mammoth 0 7497 2384 X

A series of stories based around the history of a Sheffield family. Eighteen-year-old Jess is about to leave for a year in France but first she gains some insight into the lives of her immediate relatives. She hears the story of Bridie and Jack, whose love keeps them together in spite of family divisions, of Dorothy's toil from the dirt of the buffing wheel and of her attempt to win the boss's son. One of the most moving stories concerns Danny, Jess's older handicapped brother, and his death. This is a collection of direct and heart-warming tales, told with enormous sincerity and skill. It demonstrates to young adults that previous generations have experienced emotional turmoils similar to theirs. The author's warm voice comes through strongly and in a spirited and moving manner.

HIGHLY COMMENDED

Janni Howker. *Isaac Campion* **(Julia MacRae) Heinemann**
Educational 0 435 12326 2; Walker 0 7445 4351 7

Another Northern England story, this time set totally in the past, apart from the opening and closing sequences where Isaac tells his story just before his death at the age of 96. Set in 1901, the book tells of the difficult relationship he has with his horsedealer father, a harsh, violent man. After the tragic death of his older brother, the ill-feeling deepens as does the bitter feud with a rival horsedealer, Clem Lacey. Isaac's father wants to master him as he does his horses but the boy proves to have a mind and heart of his own. This is a passionate tale of hatred and of the suffocating relationships between family members. It graphically describes the bleak world of hard-driven people.

COMMENDED

Bernard Ashley. *Running scared* (Julia MacRae) Puffin 0 14 037307 1

Another gritty novel set in the East End of London. After a jewellery raid, stolen items are left in old Sam Prescott's taxi which he elects to keep for himself. However, Charlie Elkin, who has carried out the robbery, begins to intimidate Sam's granddaughter, Paula, and puts her long-standing friendship with Narinder at risk. Narinder's family is also under Charlie Elkin's thumb and it is up to the two girls to try to unravel the clues and to take the next step in bringing Elkin to justice. This is a strong and powerful book, uncompromising in its attitude to petty criminals.

Gillian Cross. *Chartbreak* (Oxford University Press) Oxford University Press 0 19 271508 9; Puffin 0 14 032458 5

This exciting novel tells of a pop band's early life. The narrator is Janis Finch, whom we first encounter as an unhappy schoolgirl deeply resentful that her mother's new boyfriend is trying to influence both their lives. A chance meeting with a pop group in a café gives her the incentive to leave home. With money taken from her mother's earnings, she travels to London to join the group as a singer. Janis's image is remoulded by the enigmatic Christie who insists she be called Finch, have her hair cropped and generally behave in an assertive way. The story is told partly through mock magazine extracts; unlike the majority of pop-based novels, *Chartbreak* has not dated. This is an original and exciting book.

Andrew Taylor. *The coal house* (Collins) Collins Educational 0 00 330054 4

An atmospheric teenage novel with a strong heroine. After her mother's death, Alison travels north to the house her father has bought near Durham. It is an old house that was once owned by the managers of a local pit. Alison and her father are soon made aware that a tragedy happened in the house at the beginning of the century when the daughter of the house died. There is also a figure watching them at night who turns out to be a recluse, disfigured in an accident, and is half-brother to the dead girl.

CARNEGIE MEDAL WINNER 1987

Susan Price. *The ghost drum* **(Faber) Faber 0 571 15340 2**

This is a strikingly original novel set in the world of semi-fantasy and written by an author who had contributed mainly realistic work until this time. In a Russian-type setting, the Czar Guidon keeps his son Safa imprisoned in a tower. Safa's sister Margaretta is plotting to succeed him and his only ally, his nurse Marien, is no match for the cruel and powerful Czar. It is up to the witch girl Chingis, who has a hut that can run on chicken legs, to listen to the messages of the ghost drum. Through its help she can hear Safa's cries across the frozen waste. Seeped in the tradition of folk tales, *The ghost drum* most successfully brings to life the perils of life in this kingdom. There are moments of pure poetry in the writing and magical events which will enchant the more sophisticated reader.

HIGHLY COMMENDED

Margaret Mahy. *Memory* **(Dent) Dent 0 460 06269 7; Puffin 0 14 037304 7**

Nineteen-year-old Jonny sets out to find Bonny, his dead sister's best friend. Instead he becomes involved with old Sophie West who lives in genteel poverty with her cats. Sophie has senile dementia and therefore has no memory. The uneasy friendship which develops between the two of them is movingly described. This is not a subject often tackled in books for young people and Jonny's frustrations and growing affection for the old character will strike chords with large numbers of readers. Unlike Margaret Mahy's two Medal winning books, this one contains no hint of the supernatural but is strikingly realistic without being portentous or didactic.

COMMENDED

Eileen Dunlop. *The house on the hill* **(Oxford University Press) Canongate 0 86241 244 7**

Philip is staying with his great aunt Jane in the dark house at the top of the hill. There is a room at the top of the stairs which has been empty for years. However, one night he and his cousin Susan see a light under the door. This is an atmospheric novel for younger teenagers, subtly and convincingly written. It is also unusual in that it has a Scottish setting.

Monica Furlong. *Wise child* **(Gollancz) Corgi 0 552 52597 9**

This remarkable book is set on the Isle of Mull in the seventh century, although its setting and period often appear to be timeless. Told through the voice of the wise child, the novel describes her adoption and training by Juniper, a white witch and pagan. The child's father is away on a long voyage when her mother uses her and scars her mentally before running away and deserting her. The child is torn between her severe life with the witch and the glamorous life of her mother who returns to reclaim her. *Wise child* is subtly drawn and told with a quiet urgency.

Michael Morpurgo. *King of the cloud forests* **(Heinemann) Mammoth 0 7497 2777 2**

This is a novel with a most unusual theme. It tells of Ashley Anderson who is forced to flee his father's mission in China when the Japanese invade. He sets off with his guardian, the enigmatic and engaging Uncle Sung. However, they become separated during a snow storm high in the remote and icy Himalayan mountains. Starving and frozen, Ashley drifts towards death. But he is rescued by a group of strange creatures that seem to worship him as a long lost god. These are the creatures known through legend as yetis. This is a most moving and imaginative book with a host of finely tuned and evocative descriptions.

CARNEGIE MEDAL WINNER 1988

Geraldine McCaughrean. *A pack of lies* **(Oxford University Press) Puffin 0 14 037305 5**

This is a very clever and innovative book with a trio of attractive central characters. Ailsa's mother owns an antique shop and when MCC Berkshire moves in with them, he changes their lives in a dramatic way. For he is an expert storyteller and as he collars each customer and spins them a different yarn, Ailsa begins to wonder what is truth and what is fiction. Is MCC really telling a pack of lies? The stories themselves are clever pastiches of a number of genres from the detective story to *grand guignol*. It requires a sophisticated reader to spot the influences of all of the stories but most readers would have fun trying to guess. Ailsa herself is a very attractive and positive character while MCC Berkshire has all the charm of a natural born cad, which many readers will find appealing. This book was never likely to be the most immediately attractive Medal winner but it is ideal for the right reader.

HIGHLY COMMENDED

Gillian Cross. *A map of nowhere* (Oxford University Press) Oxford University Press 0 19 271583 6; Heinemann Educational 0 435 12435 8; Mammoth 0 7497 1510 3

1988 produced the longest list of Highly Commended titles in the Medal's history but it would be difficult to deny this excellent book's inclusion in that list. It uses the popularity of adventure gaming as its major theme and is both a tense thriller and a perceptive commentary on family ties and personal loyalty. Nick is of an age when being part of a gang is important. He envies his elder brother who is part of a motorcycle gang and when an opportunity arises to help this group, Nick jumps at it. He is told to infiltrate a family who own a shop the gang wishes to burgle. The way in is through adventure gaming, which the children of the shop's family, Joseph and Ruth, enjoy playing. However, Nick finds his loyalties and principles are stretched as he becomes aware of the true feelings of the family. This is a most powerful and intriguing work, providing opportunities for the reader to think about decisions the characters have to make.

Peter Dickinson. *Eva* (Gollancz) Corgi 0 552 52609 6; Longman 0 582 10159 X

This futuristic novel begins with Eva waking in hospital after a road accident. She is connected up to a complicated piece of equipment which has helped save her life by providing her with transplants from a chimpanzee, which means she looks like one and can only speak through the aid of a talking box. Her mother staunchly supports her while her father, a scientist, feels it will be an opportunity to explore the world of the apes. This is a highly original and powerfully told novel which also raises questions about the moral rights of animals.

Elizabeth Laird. *Red sky in the morning* **(Heinemann) Heinemann 0 435 94714 8; Heinemann Educational 0 435 12355 6; Pan 0 330 30890 4**

Twelve-year-old Anna is looking forward to the birth of her new baby brother but his birth is premature and he is born disabled. She still loves him and tries to look after him but there are other pressures in her life, such as the behaviour of two of her friends and the reactions to a first job. She also falls in love for the first time but, when a major crisis occurs in the family, she has to decide where her priorities lie. This is a moving and credible book written with skill and great sympathy.

COMMENDED

Vivien Alcock. *The monster garden* **(Methuen) Heinemann Educational 0 435 12349 1; Mammoth 0 7497 1706 8**

Vivien Alcock is the author of a variety of novels, often tinged with magic in some way. Frankie steals some living tissue from a laboratory and watches it grow and change in a hutch at the bottom of her garden. This is a novel for younger readers so some of the weightier moral issues associated with such an action are balanced by the excitement of creating new life. Things do not go particularly to plan but the author's account of the growing relationship between Frankie and her monster makes for fascinating and enjoyable reading.

Judy Allen. *Awaiting developments* **(Julia MacRae) Walker 0 7445 1321 9**

Winner of both the Whitbread Award and the Earthworm Award, this attractive novel takes property development as its theme. Jo's secret haven is the beautiful garden of the Big House nearby. When she hears that it has been sold to a property developer, she is determined to try to stop any building. However, as a naturally timid girl she has to try to change her habits in order to get neighbourhood support. A provocative and warm book with an appealing heroine.

Diana Wynne Jones. *The lives of Christopher Chant* **(Methuen) Mammoth 0 7497 0033 5**

Another magical title from this highly skilled writer. Christopher Chant often makes trips to the Twelve Related Worlds until his uncle Ralph learns of it and sends him on a series of missions. On one of these it is discovered that Christopher has nine lives and is thus destined to become the next Chrestomanci, the most powerful magician in the land. The young man goes to study at Chrestomanci Castle but even there he is not safe from the forces of evil. A magical yarn, rollickingly told.

CARNEGIE MEDAL WINNER 1989

Anne Fine. *Goggle-eyes* **(Hamish Hamilton) Puffin 0 14 034071 8, 0 14 036512 5**

Anne Fine is highly skilled at showing domestic situations in a fresh and mordant light. This allows her to tackle controversial situations like divorce and the arrival of step-parents in a non-threatening manner. *Goggle-eyes* shows her skill in abundance. Kitty describes her mother's new boyfriend, Gerald Faulkner, as Goggle Eyes; to her he not only stands for everything she hates but, worst of all, the other family members adore him. Kitty describes her story to Helly while they are in the school lost-property cupboard, as Helly is suffering the same problems. It is through telling the saga of what happens to Kitty's family that she helps Helly come to terms with the situation. Anne Fine is too good a writer to give a one-sided picture and, very cleverly, although always on the side of her young narrator, she manages to show the vulnerability of all the characters, both young and old. Told with sensitivity and humour, the story discusses serious issues such as jealousy, fear and even nuclear disarmament in a way that is not too obvious to the reader, who will be enjoying the story.

HIGHLY COMMENDED

Anne Fine. *Bill's new frock* **(Methuen) Mammoth 0 7497 0305 9, 0 7497 1825 0; Methuen 0 416 12152 7**

Anne Fine's novel for younger readers, *Bill's new frock*, is a farce about sex roles. Bill wakes up one morning to find that he has become a girl. Although this does not seem to surprise anyone, he learns from first-hand experience how girls are treated. They are expected to be passive, they get less space to play in, they are used as messengers, they are supposed to stay clean and they cannot beat boys at anything. However, they also get more sympathy and are less likely to get into trouble because of their misbehaviour. Bill also uses the opportunity to get back at the bullies who have been plaguing him. Plenty of food for thought but also a rollicking good read.

Carole Lloyd. *The Charlie Barber treatment* (Julia MacRae)

This fine novel has death as its main theme but it is very much life-affirming. Simon arrives home from school to find his beloved mother dead beside her bed. The effect this has on the family is described with great warmth and understanding. With the help of his friend Kevin, Simon returns to school and although outwardly calm, his grief and the disintegrating home life with his father mean that he is unable to become involved in anything and his schoolwork suffers. Then one day he comes across the outgoing Charlie Barber whose attitude to life helps Simon to come to terms with his grief and to try to forge a relationship with his father. This is a positive and sympathetic book on a taboo subject which will make young adults aware of the feelings their peers have when bereaved.

COMMENDED

Vivien Alcock. *The trial of Anna Cotman* (Methuen)

In this story about gangs, shy Anna is discovered by Lindy Miller and is introduced to a colourful world of secret codes and dressing up which contrasts sharply with Anna's drab existence. However, the glamour does not hide the folly of an intrinsically corrupt group of young people; when Anna makes her stand against it, it occurs naturally and not through any false heroics on her part. She prevails almost by chance but also with adult help which provides a suitable ending to this sombre but extremely powerful novel.

CARNEGIE MEDAL WINNER 1990

Gillian Cross. *Wolf* (Oxford University Press) Puffin 0 14 034826 3

Wolves have long fascinated writers of work for young people from folk tales onwards. Gillian Cross very cleverly combines the fear and admiration many have for these creatures with feelings towards modern terrorists. Cassy lives with her grandmother but each time a secret visitor appears, she is sent away to stay with her mother in a succession of squats. Goldie, Cassy's mother, is a childlike woman whose latest lover is the black and quietly powerful Lyall. Together with Lyall's sensible teenage son, Robert, they have formed a theatre-in-education drama company and their latest project is a presentation on wolves. Reluctantly Cassie is persuaded to join them, discovering more about the animals as her research progresses. She also discovers that her mysterious father was fascinated by wolves too but she later learns that there is a far greater secret involving her father, who is a member of the IRA and who threatens Cassie's grandmother's life unless some lost Semtex is returned to him. *Wolf* is a subtle and powerful book which can be read on a number of levels.

HIGHLY COMMENDED

Melvin Burgess. *The cry of the wolf* (Andersen Press) Andersen 0 86264 308 2; Puffin 0 14 037318 7

Another wolf novel and a powerful and uncompromising one from a writer who has made a considerable impact on these awards in recent years. The sinister Hunter sees his mission in life as exterminiating any remaining wolves from England. Ten-year-old Ben is an exterminator of smaller animals such as birds and he tells the Hunter that there is still a wolf pack left in Surrey. The reader is not sure if indeed the Hunter has been produced by Ben's imagination. The wolf pack is led by Silver, and her Greycub is the animal that turns the Hunter into the Hunted. This is an arresting and unusual novel for those with strong stomachs.

Robert Westall. *The kingdom by the sea* (Methuen) Heinemaan Educational 0 435 12392 0; Mammoth 0 7497 0796 8

Winner of the *Guardian* Award, Robert Westall's novel is a realistic and painful account of domestic life in the Second World War. Harry's house has been bombed and it appears his parents have lost their lives. He doesn't want to be sent away to Cousin Elsie's home so he runs away. He is a survivor and, along with Don the dog, another stray, roams the bombed-out areas of the North East of England. He is befriended by Mr M who helps to locate his parents. The final reunion with them is not a happy one and one thing Harry has learnt on his adventures is that he has the resourcefulness to survive what life throws at him. A powerful and touching book which lifts the veil off a rose-tinted view of the war period.

COMMENDED

Theresa Tomlinson. *Riding the waves* **(Julia MacRae) Walker
0 7445 2312 5**

Matt worships the surf-riders who ride the waves but is unable to join them, much as he would like to. Against his better judgment, he befriends Florrie, an elderly woman whom he has interviewed for a history project. Through her he learns the history of his town and she helps him to come to terms with the fact that he is adopted. Florrie also helps him to achieve his ambition to become a surf rider although he finds it is much harder work than he expected. This is a warm and sympathetic novel which touches on a number of important issues in a winning way.

CARNEGIE MEDAL WINNER 1991

Berlie Doherty. *Dear nobody* **(Hamish Hamilton) Hamilton
0 241 13056 5; Lions 0 00 674618 7**

This was a controversial choice because its main theme is teenage pregnancy. Written partly in letter form by Helen to her unborn baby, it describes the first flush of romance which is followed by the horrifying discovery of Helen's pregnancy. Deeply unhappy, she determines to break off her relationship but Chris, the father, feels he should have some say in the baby's future. Confronted with the possibility of themselves becoming parents, they struggle with the feelings of their own parents. Helen discovers that her mother was born illegitimate. She refuses to have an abortion or to give the baby up for adoption but there is still hope that she can have a positive future, either with or without Chris. This is a mature and deeply sympathetic book, touching on a controversial topic in a non-judgmental way. As with her previous Award winner, *Granny was a buffer girl*, the past is often portrayed as impinging on the present.

HIGHLY COMMENDED

Jacqueline Wilson. *The story of Tracy Beaker* **(Doubleday)
Yearling 0 440 86279 5**

Tracy Beaker is a winning heroine and her story is far from the conventional middle-class norm of much writing for children. She lives in a children's home but she manages to escape in her mind through the use of her writing. She attempts to hide her vulnerability behind a facade of not caring but it is often obvious how much she cares about her family and her surroundings. The reader can easily empathize with her aspirations and her attitude to life while also, through the skill of the writing, being aware of the realities of her situation. When the happy ending comes, it does not seem to strike a false note.

COMMENDED

Annie Dalton. *The real Tilly Beany* **(Methuen) Mammoth 0 7497 0983 9**

This is a collection of stories for younger children. Five-year-old Matilda Beany, the youngest of four, wants to be different. She invents a number of different personas for herself which her long-suffering family accepts. However, when they find Cindertilly scrubbing their doorstep, they wonder if perhaps she has not taken things a little too far. This is a warm and skilfully crafted collection of stories which beginner readers slightly older than Tilly herself will regard with fond amusement.

Garry Kilworth. *The drowners* **(Methuen) Methuen 0 416 17682 8; Mammoth 0 7497 1049 7**

This is both an historical novel and a ghost story which combines both genres with success. Set at the beginning of the nineteenth century, its premise is a method whereby farmers drown their land at a certain time to produce better crops. This is an old tradition and Tim, the apprentice Master Drowner, is murdered by the henchman of the jealous landlord, Sir Francis. After the death of the Master Drowner, there is noone who can carry on the tradition and the crops and season fail dramatically. The ghost of Tim returns to help the villagers and the landlord and his thugs are brought to justice.

CARNEGIE MEDAL WINNER 1992

Anne Fine. *Flour babies* **(Hamish Hamilton) Hamilton 0 241 13252 5; Longman 0 582 29259 X; Puffin 0 14 036147 2**

Another mordant Anne Fine novel, based on a true experiment. Mr Cartright has decided that his pupils will try something a little different for the annual school science fair. They are each presented with six pound bags of flour which they have to treat as if they were real babies. Simon approaches this with the lack of enthusiasm he gives to most school projects. There is a good deal of amusement to be gained from his attempts to look after the creature and his numerous threats to give up. However, the project and the book do have a serious purpose: to get young people thinking about the role of parenthood. Simon realizes why his mother often gets cross with him and it also helps him to realize how his father must have felt when he deserted the family. Simon (and hopefully the reader, particularly the male one) emerges at the end of the book a more rounded person, while also being able to laugh at the situations which this clever and witty writer sets up.

HIGHLY COMMENDED

Robert Westall. *Gulf* (Methuen) Heinemann Educational 0 435 12414 5; Mammoth 0 7497 1472 7

A short and original book, *Gulf* is one of the few books to have the Gulf War as its theme. The narrator is Tom who is protective of his younger, more sensitive brother Figgis. When Figgis is taken over by Larif, a young conscript in Saddam's army, the doctors are baffled until Dr Rashid takes on the case. He recognizes that Figgis is speaking in Arabic and is able to help him. This is a thought-provoking book, scathing in its attack on war and its effect on young people, and powerfully written.

COMMENDED

Gillian Cross. *The great elephant chase* (Oxford University Press) Oxford University Press 0 19 271725 1; Puffin 0 14 036361 0

In contrast, this is a rollicking picaresque novel told with great good humour and flair. Set in nineteenth-century America, it describes how Tad, an orphan, gets trapped in the elephant box of a travelling troupe and is employed by Keenan, the elephant's owner. After a train crash, Tod and Keenan's daughter Cissie are left with the elephant. A figure from Tod's past, Mr Jackson, appears and claims that Khush, the elephant, had been sold to him and there then begins a furious chase across America as the pair meet a collection of unusual characters. This tale is splendidly told with warm and sympathetic characterization.

Peter Dickinson. *A bone from a dry sea* **(Gollancz) Corgi 0 552 52797 1**

This is a typically uncompromising novel from Peter Dickinson, set in two worlds: the first a contemporary setting and the other a world at the beginning of evolution. Vinny is with her father on an expedition in Africa which is looking for evidence of early humans. Her counterpart is Li whose race is beginning to emerge from a succession of apes and who is starting to think with reason and an underlying spiritual dimension. The two lives intertwine until the reader is unaware which is which. Dickinson's imagination and depth of writing in crafting this book are unparalleled.

CARNEGIE MEDAL WINNER 1993

Robert Swindells. *Stone cold* **(Hamish Hamilton) Heinemann Educational 0 435 12468 4; Puffin 0 14 036251 7**

This choice and some of the other books on the awards list created a good deal of media controversy as the judges were accused of selecting only books which examine the darker side of life. *Stone cold* does indeed have as its theme two important aspects of modern life: homelessness and serial killers. Link escapes his abusive stepfather to live on the streets of London. He is a complete novice and it is only through the help of other street dwellers, particularly his friend Ginger, that he is able to scrape a living. There is a further danger to the lives of those living on the streets. This is a serial killer who calls himself Shelter and whose diary entries run parallel with Link's own story. The serial killer who is an ex-army man writes chillingly of how he is attempting to rid his world of those such as Link and his friends, who he regards as scum. Ginger becomes Shelter's latest victim but Link is distracted by the appearance of Gail, who is not what she at first appears to be. The inevitable confrontation between Link and Shelter draws the book to a chilling climax. This is a powerful novel, uncompromising in its attitude towards both of its themes and with a deeply strong anger at the causes of the homelessness of Link and so many other young people like him.

HIGHLY COMMENDED

Melvin Burgess. *The baby and Fly Pie* **(Andersen Press) Andersen 0 86264 461 5; Puffin 0 14 036982 1**

Another novel about homelessness but this time a much bleaker one. Set in the future, it tells of Shaun, Fly Pie and his sister Jane who are homeless and live on a large encampment. They make a living out of petty thieving but when they find a baby on a tip which they discover belongs to a rich family, they decide to hold it for ransom for £17 million, which has been stolen. Their futile attempts to look after the child and the ambush which lies in wait for them when they attempt to return it are told with great power and skill. The atmosphere of the setting is, however, terrifyingly nihilistic and the ending gives little cause for optimism.

Jenny Nimmo. *The stone mouse* **(Walker) Walker 0 7445 3186 1**

This is a great contrast with the other books on the list and is intended for a younger audience. Elly has conversations with the stone mouse, much to her brother Ted's disgust. He attempts to get rid of the creature by throwing it in the sea but the stone mouse survives and eventually helps Ted by becoming his friend too. The themes in the book – sibling rivalry, the relationship between parents and children, the importance of friends – are delicately touched upon in a warm-hearted and approachable way.

COMMENDED

Anne Merrick. *Someone came knocking* **(Spindlewood) Spindlewood 0 907349 32 3; Puffin 0 14 037136 2**

In this most successful first novel, Tod is a boy whose memories of the past have been erased by the horrors of his present life with his father. He escapes from his home with his companion, an eerily talking large rag doll called Mim. After a long search and a number of nail-biting adventures, his recollections of an earlier life return to him and he is able to make contact with a significant family member. This is a story beautifully and powerfully presented by a writer with an assured touch.

CARNEGIE MEDAL WINNER 1994

Theresa Breslin. *Whispers in the graveyard* **(Methuen)**
Heinemann Educational 0 435 12470 6; Mammoth 0 7497 2388 2

A combination of an issues novel and a ghost story, *Whispers in the graveyard* succeeds in both areas. Solomon is full of anger, with his father and with his school because he feels he cannot learn, and with his mother for deserting him. His only refuge is at the corner of a local graveyard. Nothing grows there except a rowan tree but when workmen begin to uproot the tree, an evil from the past, speaking to Solomon through ghostly voices, is unleashed. The ghostly element is very powerful, creating a tangible shudder in the reader. The other important aspect of Solomon's life is that he is dyslexic and when this is diagnosed, his life begins to take on a different dimension. The link between the seventeenth century witch hunts and Solomon's very modern status as an outsider is cleverly portrayed and despite its sombre setting, there is still a good deal of optimism in the book.

HIGHLY COMMENDED

Berlie Doherty. *Willa and old Miss Annie* **(Walker) Walker 0 7445 2402 4, 0 7445 3684 7**

This is a charming collection of stories for the younger reader. When Willa first meets Miss Annie she is afraid of her, for the old woman has woolly hair, a tiny voice and bumpy hands. However, they soon form a deep friendship when they discover that they have in common a love of animals. The three stories each revolve around a particular animal: a goat, a pony and a fox. *Willa and old Miss Annie* is a warm and very human collection which shows the abiding friendship of two people at different ends of the age range.

Lesley Howarth. *MapHead* **(Walker) Walker 0 744 54141 7, 0 744 53647 2**

This is an unusual and original novel. Powers and his 12-year-old son Boothe (known as MapHead because he can flash up a map of any place across his head) are visitors from the Subtle World. MapHead has come to earth to meet his human mother for the first time. He and his father make their temporary home in a tomato hothouse from where MapHead can explore the extraordinary lives of human beings. This is a world which soon draws in the reader until it becomes a totally credible situation.

MapHead's emotions are large and we become as involved with them in a subtle and exciting way.

CARNEGIE MEDAL WINNER 1995

Philip Pullman. *His dark materials 1. Northern lights* **(Scholastic) Point 0 590 54178 1, 0 590 13961 4**

His dark materials is one of the most significant trilogies in twentieth century children's literature. Both highly readable and deeply intelligent and imaginative, *Northern lights* begins the saga of a world similar to modern Britain but with significant differences. It is a world of academics where all humans carry with them a daemon which changes shape according to its owner's mood and where a team of scientists is examining the dust which surrounds the bodies of children. The splendidly adventurous heroine, Lyra, finds herself drawn into the quest to discover the reason for the experiments which are being carried out on the children to cut them off from their daemons, all the time fighting the villainy of her persuasively glamorous mother. Underlying all this is the theme of religious superstition versus scientific rationality, supported by a multitude of strongly drawn characters. *Northern lights*, thick with literary illusions (the title of the trilogy is drawn from *Paradise lost*), wears its intelligence lightly and creates a totally credible milieu into which the reader is subtly drawn.

HIGHLY COMMENDED

Jacqueline Wilson. *Double act* **(Doubleday) Doubleday 0 385 40537 5; Yearling 0 440 86334 1**

Jacqueline Wilson is highly skilled at drawing modern issues into very readable and witty novels. *Double act* is told through the eyes of twins, Ruby and Garnet, physically similar but, as so often in real life, different in character. Ruby is the leader of the two, particularly after the death of their mother. Their world changes dramatically when their father's new girlfriend, Rose, wants them all to move in together. How the girls, in their own different ways, cope with change is told with quirky humour. The author has a wonderful knack of getting under the skin of her characters and of being totally convincing in the way she tells the girls' stories through their own words. The book is skilfully produced (two different artists are used for each of the twins) and attractively child-centred.

COMMENDED

Susan Gates. *Raider* (Oxford University Press) Oxford University Press 0 19 271644 1, 0 19 271752 9

A novel which shows the hardship of fishing life, both past and present. Two dissimilar girls, Maddy and Flora, are paired together for a school project. They unearth a mystery of 40 years previously which involved the trawler, the Arctic Raider. The conclusion brings them closer together and changes both of them for the better. An atmospheric and involving novel which depicts the reality of life on a trawler.

CARNEGIE MEDAL WINNER 1996

Melvin Burgess. *Junk* (Andersen Press) Andersen 0 86264 632 4; Puffin 0 14 038019 1

This novel, which takes drug addiction as its theme, is possibly the most controversial winner of the Carnegie Medal in its history. Definitely intended for a mature audience, it also won the *Guardian* Award. Two teenagers, Tar and Gemma, leave their homes to escape their respective situations. They become involved in the world of soft drugs, move on to the harsher world of heroin addiction and encounter prostitution and prison. The motif which runs through the book is, in the words of one addict, 'we can move off this stuff any time we like'. Set in the 1980s, this is a very moral book which would discourage any teenager who had read the whole book from taking drugs. The narrative employs the words of 14 characters, which helps to present a number of differing viewpoints. One could question the length but it is difficult to dispute the powerful effect *Junk* has on the reader.

HIGHLY COMMENDED

Anne Fine. *The Tulip touch* (Hamish Hamilton) Hamish Hamilton 0 241 13578 8; Puffin 0 14 037808 1

Inspired by a notorious child abduction case, Anne Fine's novel displays all the skills to be expected from this talented writer. Natalie, who feels her life is dull, becomes friendly with the enigmatic Tulip whose home life is sketched in deliberately lightly. The reader is aware that there could well be abuse in the family but a writer as subtle as Anne Fine does not force this issue. Tulip's efforts to attract attention become more and more extreme until Natalie is forced to seriously examine their relationship. Winner also of the Whitbread Award, *The Tulip touch* succeeds because the writer does not portray Tulip as a complete monster but allows the reader to glimpse something of what makes her the person she is.

COMMENDED

Terry Pratchett. *Johnny and the bomb* (Doubleday) Doubleday 0 385 4 670 3; Corgi 0 552 52968 0

Johnny Maxwell and his friends, who have appeared in two previous Pratchett titles *Only you can save mankind* and *Johnny and the dead*, return in this time slip story in which they travel to 1940s London. The catalyst is Mrs Tachyon, the bag lady, one of the author's most appealing and distinctive characters. This humorous and thought-provoking novel is told in Terry Pratchett's typically droll manner.

The Kate Greenaway Medal

Winners and commended titles

1955: NO AWARD WAS MADE FOR THIS YEAR

KATE GREENAWAY MEDAL WINNER 1956

Edward Ardizzone. *Tim all alone* **(Oxford University Press)**

It could be no surprise that Ardizzone was the first winner of this Medal. He had made such a significant contribution to illustrated books in previous decades that his contribution was bound to be rewarded. *Tim all alone* is quintessential Ardizzone. Tim comes home after a seaside holiday to find his home deserted and with a 'To let' sign above it. He joins a ship's company and visits many ports to find his parents. There is a violent storm at sea, graphically depicted by the artist, and Tim is washed up on shore whereupon he is reunited with his parents. Obviously the storyline is fantasy but one can imagine its general theme raising a number of eyebrows in adult readers. Ardizzone's familiar chunky figures and his delicate use of colour washes make this a highly attractive book but it is unlikely to appeal to young readers used to a more sophisticated style of presentation or a less complex manner of telling stories.

KATE GREENAWAY MEDAL WINNER 1957

V. H. Drummond. *Mrs Easter and the storks* **(Faber)**

Violet Drummond's illustrations are very much of the period: charming line drawings with a somewhat insubstantial and almost ethereal definition. Mrs Easter and Billie Guftie mean to return from Denmark on board the S.S. Queenie but they find themselves travelling on the back of Sam the stork. There is far more text and smaller drawings than those used to modern picture books would expect, with half the book in black and white and half in colour. It is unlikely this book would appeal without the assistance of an adult mediator but it does have a good deal of charm and could create discussion about the different techniques used by picture-book artists of the day and modern practitioners.

1958: NO AWARD WAS MADE FOR THIS YEAR

KATE GREENAWAY MEDAL WINNER 1959

William Stobbs. *A bundle of ballads* [text compiled by Ruth Manning-Sanders] (Oxford University Press)

Kashtanka [text by Anton Chekhov] (Oxford University Press)

Stobbs had a long career as an artist, retaining his strong position as a superb technician but also adapting his techniques according to the style of the period. These are both early works where the technician is to the fore, particularly in the first book where his line drawings, sometimes washed with brown, add attractive decoration to this varied collection of minstrel songs. *Kashtanka* is adapted from a story by the famous Russian playwright. The eponymous heroine is a dog who, out on a walk with her carpenter owner, is frightened by the noise of a soldier band. She runs off and is taken in by a stranger, a circus performer. She shares her life with a cat, a gander and a pig and at the story's climax has to choose between the glamour of her new life and her life with the carpenter. There is much more text than is usual in modern picture books and most of the book consists of black-and-white line drawings with the occasional coloured picture.

COMMENDED

Edward Ardizzone. *Titus in trouble* [text by James Reeves] (Bodley Head)

Titus is a small boy from the Victorian period who wants to go to sea. First he has to find £10 to pay for some vases he has broken. He tries one job after another until a final breakage gives him the impetus to set off for sea. Reeves' text, strongly constructed, is ably supported by Ardizzone's atmospheric illustrations, particularly in the scenes set in a grimy railway station and on the London docks.

Gerald Rose. *Wuffles goes to town* [text with Elizabeth Rose] (Faber)

This picture book is told with vigour and humour. A visit to town by Wuffles, a dog with a wonderful nose, ends in an exciting chase through the streets of London pursuing a thief. Rose's delightful illustrations are full of character.

KATE GEENAWAY MEDAL WINNER 1960

Gerald Rose. *Old Winkle and the seagulls* [text by Elizabeth Rose] (Faber)

Gerald Rose's cartoon-like illustrations enhance and enliven this jolly picture book. Old Winkle is a fisherman who is friendly with the birds but generally unlucky with his fishing. A fish shortage enhances his relationship with the birds as they tell him where to fish. There is still far less colour than we are used to in modern picture books (exactly half the book is in black-and-white) but the expanse of colour when it does arrive makes a distinct impression.

KATE GREENAWAY MEDAL WINNER 1961

Anthony Maitland. *Mrs Cockle's cat* [text by Philippa Pearce] (Longman) Puffin 0 14 032118 7

Anthony Maitland's distinctive and often powerfully evocative drawings, which have graced a number of books, can be seen at their best in his line drawings for Leon Garfield's novels. This still popular picture book with a long narrative tells of a London balloon-seller who is swept away to a seaside village where she meets her cat. The rollicking style of both the text and the illustrations, with its mixture of black-and-white and colour images, makes this an enjoyable read.

KATE GREENAWAY MEDAL WINNER 1962

Brian Wildsmith. *ABC* (Oxford University Press) Star Bright 1 887734 02 3

Wildsmith was one of the artists to use to the full new techniques in colour printing being developed at this time, helped by the foresight of his publishers, Oxford University Press. In this alphabet book he produces a riot of colour matched with his distinctively drawn portrayals of animals and other objects. Look at the blaze of colour shown by the butterfly drawn against a dark background. The fierce jaguar is instantly recognizable and the final image in the book, a zebra with its back to the reader, is beautifully characterized. Images like this would not have been possible when the Kate Greenaway Medal was first introduced and although refinements were produced in later years, this is still the image that many people remember when thinking of picture books.

COMMENDED

Carol Barker. *Achilles the donkey* [text by H.E.Bates] (Dobson)

A donkey sold to an old man on Mykonos runs way from his harsh treatment to find a good home with an affectionate family. The pictures are Grecian in concept with subtle colours and a formal style. They are almost frieze-like in their decorative quality.

KATE GREENAWAY MEDAL WINNER 1963

John Burningham. *Borka* (Cape) Cape 0 224 60077 X; Red Fox 0 09 989910 8

John Burningham is still producing books of such high quality that it is difficult to remember that he has had such a long career. His illustrative style has changed in some ways over the years but his drawings are still recognizably Burningham. His illustrations in *Borka* are much bolder than in his later work, particularly his other Greenaway Medal winner, *Mr Gumpy's outing*. Borka is a goose with no feathers. She is teased by the other members of her flock because she cannot fly. She is adopted by a ship's crew and makes friends with the highly individual dog called Fowler, eventually ending up in Kew Gardens. This is a hugely enjoyable romp with an attractive heroine and a series of appealing supporting characters, strongly drawn and using more colour than previous Medal winners.

COMMENDED

Victor Ambrus. *The Royal Navy* [text by Peter Dawlish] (Oxford University Press)

Victor Ambrus. *Time of trial* [text by Hester Burton] (Oxford University Press)

Ambrus is another illustrator with a long career as his strongly and skilfully drawn portraits are still gracing new publications. He is particularly